524

KUTUUKA

(to reach)

A collection of photographs, dreams and drawings
benefitting Change the Truth

Yellow Bird Press, 2009

www.gloriabakerfeinstein.com

Printed in the United States of America

ISBN 0-9719487-2-0

Designed by Lindsay Laricks, Kansas City, Missouri
Printed by Meridian Printing, East Greenwich, Rhode Island
Bound at ACME Bookbinding, Charlestown, Massachusetts
Typeset in Trade Gothic
Printed on Topkote

....

This book is dedicated to the children in Uganda
who have broadened my understanding of joy and sorrow
and who have taught me about hope.

....

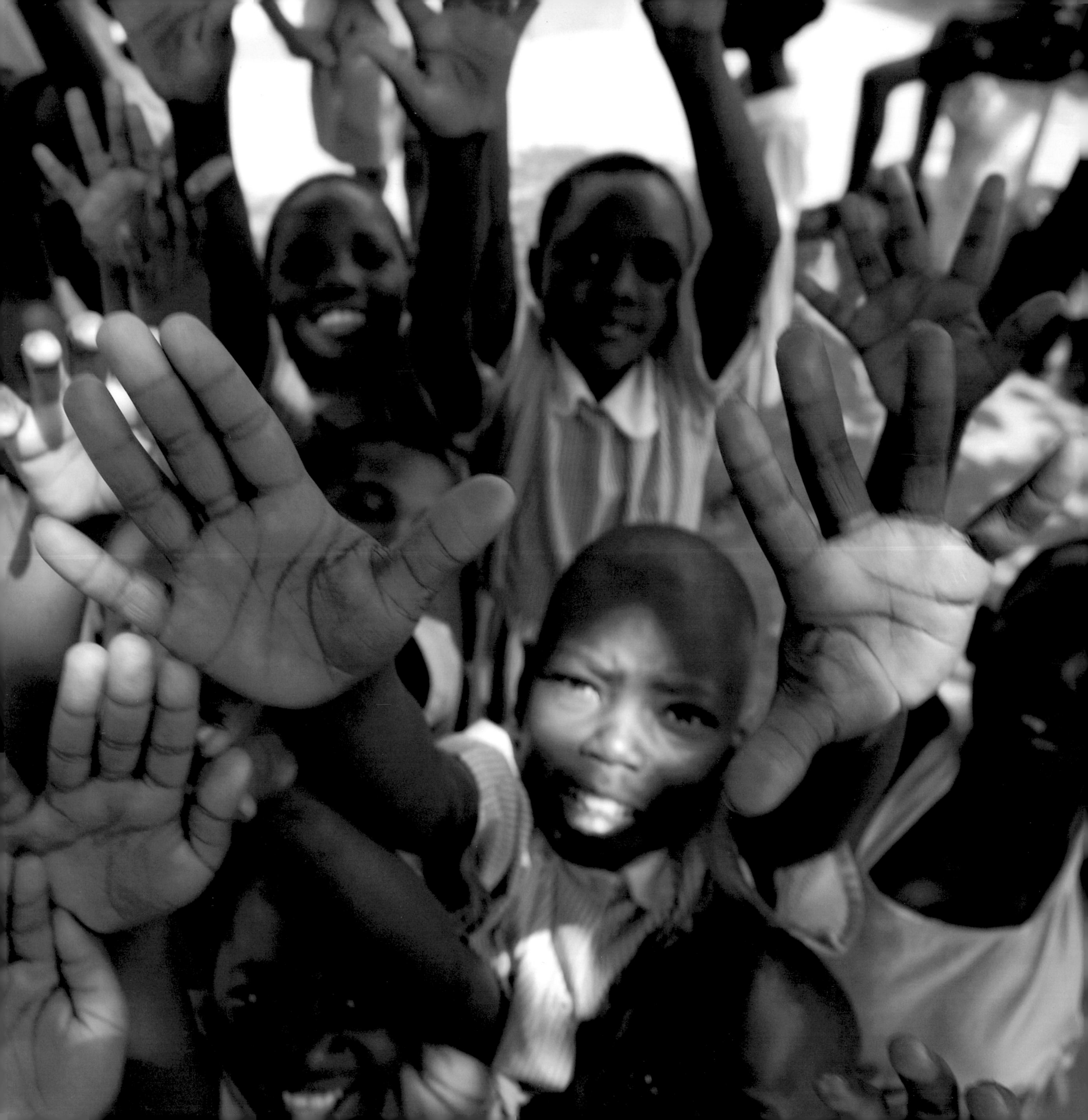

GLORIA BAKER FEINSTEIN

Uganda is a developing nation. Water and electricity go out at odd hours. The roads are bad, things do not happen on schedule, and the food can make your stomach rebel. Petty crime is rampant. A civil war makes the northern part of the country unsafe. Health risks include HIV/AIDS, malaria and yellow fever.

Even so, in November 2006 I packed my gear and boarded a flight for Entebbe, near Uganda's capital.

....

There are over two million orphans in Uganda. Some roam the streets—ragged, dirty, haunted, with their palms reaching out for a spare coin or two. Some live with aunts, grandmothers or neighbors, who often struggle to keep families together. Some find their way to an orphanage.

I soon got to know many of these children. I found myself deeply saddened by the heart-wrenching stories they told me, the torn clothing they wore, the dirty water they drank, and the diseases and poverty that surrounded them and threatened to circumscribe their young lives.

I was there to make pictures, though, which was a good thing. I have always felt comforted when putting a frame around, and thus isolating, the things that I see. In doing so, I remove myself somewhat from the reality at hand, but I also bring myself closer to it so that I can linger on it, study it, consider it and try to make sense of it.

This critical distance was exactly what was called for as I made my way from orphanage to small village to displaced persons camp in the stifling air and gritty dust of Uganda.

I was taking a workshop, learning how to make pictures for non-governmental organizations. My self-assigned project was to photograph AIDS and war orphans. Eventually, trying to make sense of what I saw asked more of me than simply making pictures. The experience changed the course of my life. Unable to forget what I had seen and heard, I started an organization that provides assistance to a large community of these orphaned children. It is called Change the Truth; we work to expand opportunities for children at Saint Mary Kevin Orphanage Motherhood (SMKOM). This endeavor has become the centerpiece of my life as a photographer.

I have traveled the pitted, red dirt road up to the orphanage many times since that first journey. Now I am accompanied by volunteers who want to help: therapists, artists, doctors and gardeners among them. What constantly amazes us about the people we meet is their strong will to survive and thrive in spite of profoundly dire circumstances.

The children at SMKOM are forever trying to teach me one of their languages, Lugandan. In honor of these young people who are never willing to give up in their attempts to help me speak their language, I have chosen Lugandan words for the title of this book and for the titles of its three sections. The first section includes photographs made during my visits to Uganda. The second represents a partnership between several of the children at SMKOM and me: I asked them to write about a dream (*kilooto*) they had when asleep at night. After working on these compositions together, the children and I undertook the task of "illustrating" that dream in a photograph. The last section comprises drawings and paintings made by the children. Each section title makes reference to the notion of reaching, an act that can be both external and internal. Whether reaching up, through or in, I believe that each of us is always searching for new and meaningful ways to connect with ourselves—and then with others.

A few meager possessions, maybe a change of clothes, perhaps a pair of shoes: that's all these children have. An unbridled spirit for living, a tremendous amount of talent and resourcefulness, a limitless capacity for love and a boundless sense of hope: that's what they have to give.

THATCHER HULLERMAN COOK

I was browsing through Tim Whelan's bookstore in Rockport, Maine, when Corbin, my girlfriend, handed me a photography book and asked me what I thought. The formal compositions were simultaneously sensitive and unsentimental: a baby's hand pointing to a bird, for example. I was immediately intrigued by the way this photographer experienced her surroundings, creating pictures that made visual sense without relying on gratuitous tricks. The beautiful and respectful images, testament to the photographer's unique perspective, stayed with me. Corbin had found a treasure.

Several months later, I found myself in Uganda teaching a photography workshop, the goal of which was to document that country's struggles with disease, poverty and war. The workshop comprised two separate but complementary experiences: first, the students would spend several days photographing the daily lives of families in the Rakai district, a place devastated by AIDS; then, traveling separately, the students would photograph programs for a non-governmental organization of their choosing.

On the first day, by way of introduction, I invited the students to share some of their work. One student, Gloria Baker Feinstein, pulled out a copy of a book called *Convergence*. Its cover image, a pudgy little hand pointing to a bird, registered immediately. I was shocked, deeply honored and a little concerned to have such an accomplished photographer as a student in my workshop. But most of all, I felt the strange connectedness between a small bookstore in Maine and a country in Africa.

....

Ugandan clouds are among the most beautiful in the world. This thought occurred to me as I waited outside while Gloria and the other workshop participants said their goodbyes to the Rakai host families. I watched the clouds through the window of our van while the driver slept in his seat. They rolled along, offering a light rain without thunder.

We had parked on a widened dirt path across from a mud shack with a corrugated tin roof. On the dirt in front of the shack sat a young girl with a shaved head and a faded blue dress. She was blind and mute, and she swayed with metronomic accuracy as if listening to an internal symphony. Rakai is known as the birthplace of AIDS. Disease had made her village silent. At least for that moment, this young girl experienced a wholly tactile world in complete isolation, absorbing the atmosphere of the day through her skin and exploring her surroundings with her fingers.

The door to the mud home opened behind the girl and without a sound, a single red balloon floated out of the dark doorway. A group of boys followed. They tapped the balloon with their fingers, the goal being to keep the balloon from touching the ground. They were quiet and respectful, making sure not to invade the blind girl's space.

I wanted to join the boys in their dance, but I refrained. The scene was beautiful, and I raised my camera to make photographs through the raindrops on the van window. The slow, silent rain became a noisy downpour. The boys ducked back under the hut's ringing roof and the red balloon fell to the earth, landing near the now-abandoned girl. She sat in the rain, her sway gathering energy as if she were on the verge of laughter. Then a young man came out, lifted her up and placed her near the exterior wall of the shack—under the overhanging eave of the roof—so that she could be protected from the rain. He quickly went back inside, leaving the girl alone to continue to rock. Inside the van the sound of the rain became a meditative white noise. The forgotten balloon lay in a growing puddle.

When the rain stopped, the workshop students emerged and boarded the van. The family that had hosted Gloria escorted her back to the bus. The boys helped her carry their farewell gift to her: a large bundle of bananas. While the other students compared stories on the road back to Kampala, Gloria sat quietly, staring towards the horizon. As I learned later, she was considering a suggestion I had offered on the first day: that the workshop was about more than building a portfolio; it was about giving a voice to the silent. The camera in her lap contained images that would help do just that.

....

Gloria's photographs represent a poetic exploration of a troubled nation rather than a simple expository documentation of a place consumed by strife and suffering. Upon their first look at Uganda, it can be very easy for outsiders to see only pain. Its violent history has left over two million children displaced by war or orphaned by AIDS. Gloria made a deliberate choice to create beauty from her experiences in the country rather than simply to document its tragedy. Never abandoning or forgetting her several roles—as a journalist, mother and artist—she photographed the everyday in a way that lets the viewer in and makes Uganda accessible. We feel no shame as we look because we recognize the people in her photographs; they play, relax, attend school and share meals just as we do. While we might be aware that some may be orphaned, without a home or afflicted by AIDS, we connect to them emotionally and feel viscerally our shared humanity.

I believe Gloria's pictures explore the intersection of the physical world with a deep internal emotional reaction, much like the blind girl in the red mud. The two have a similar intuitive and spiritual response to their environment: the young girl uses her fingers to feel and interpret her surroundings, whereas Gloria uses her lens.

Gloria's Uganda portfolio is a departure in some ways from the previous work that caught my attention on that day in Maine. These less formal images are more instinctive, full of movement and transition. They resonate with an energy that I believe is essentially African. Instead of focusing on surfaces, this body of work explores the interdependency of layers. Gloria's thoughtful work reveals the dignity and soulful beauty of the people of Uganda and helps us feel our connectedness to an often-overlooked corner of the world.

Thatcher Hullerman Cook is a documentary photographer based in Maine. His clients are humanitarian relief and development organizations that work with people affected by war, economic upheaval and natural disasters.

TUUKA WAGGULU

(reach up)

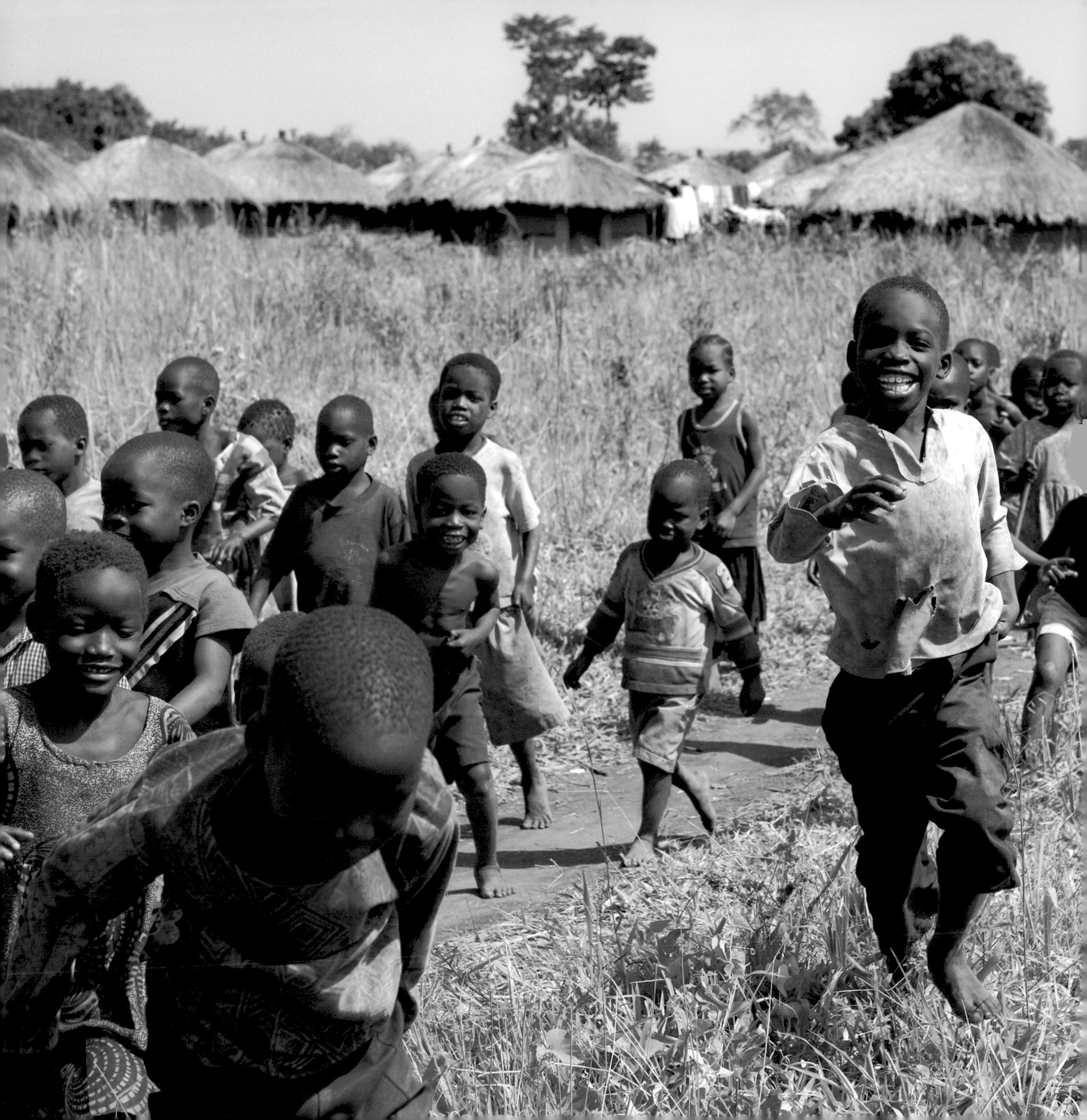

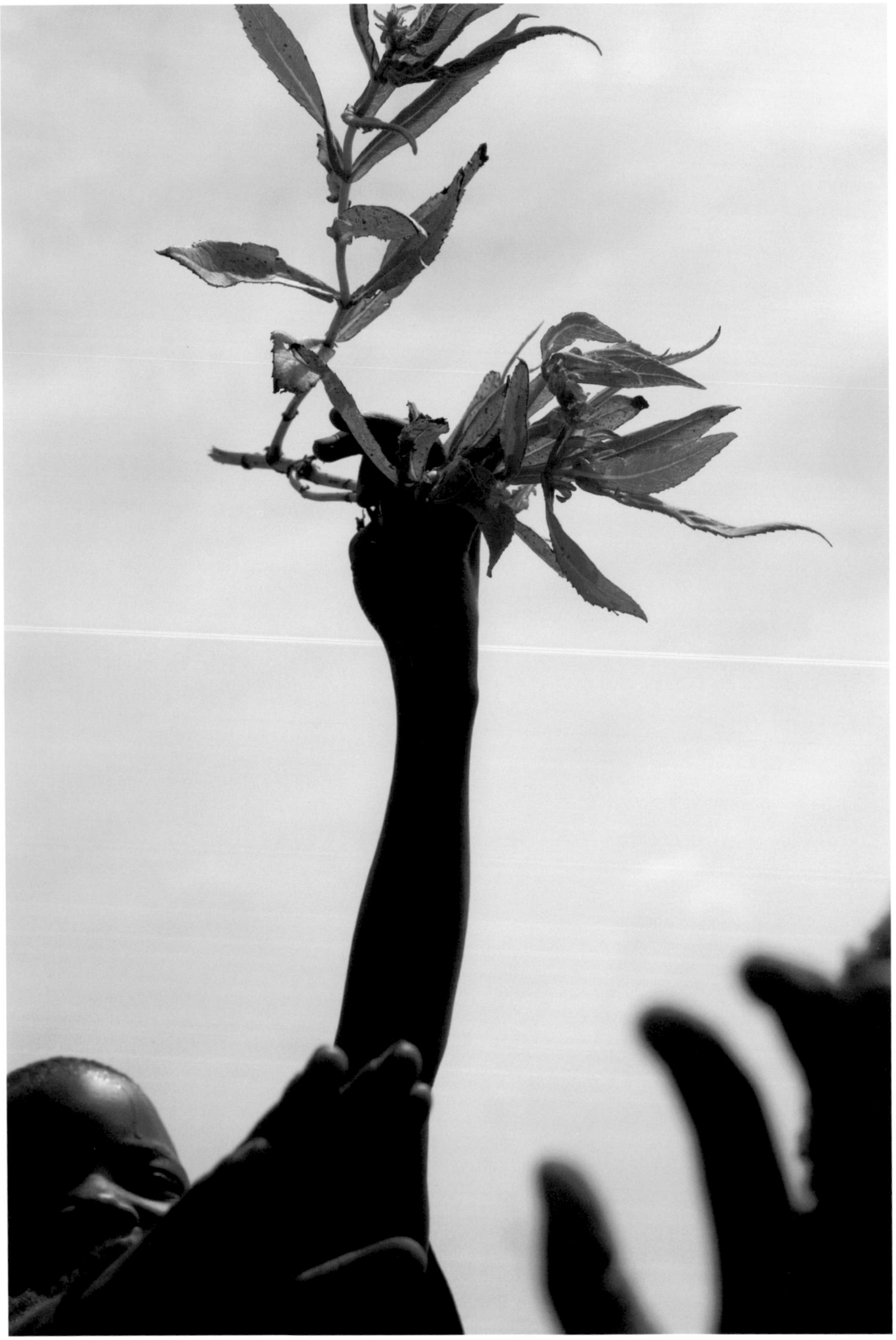

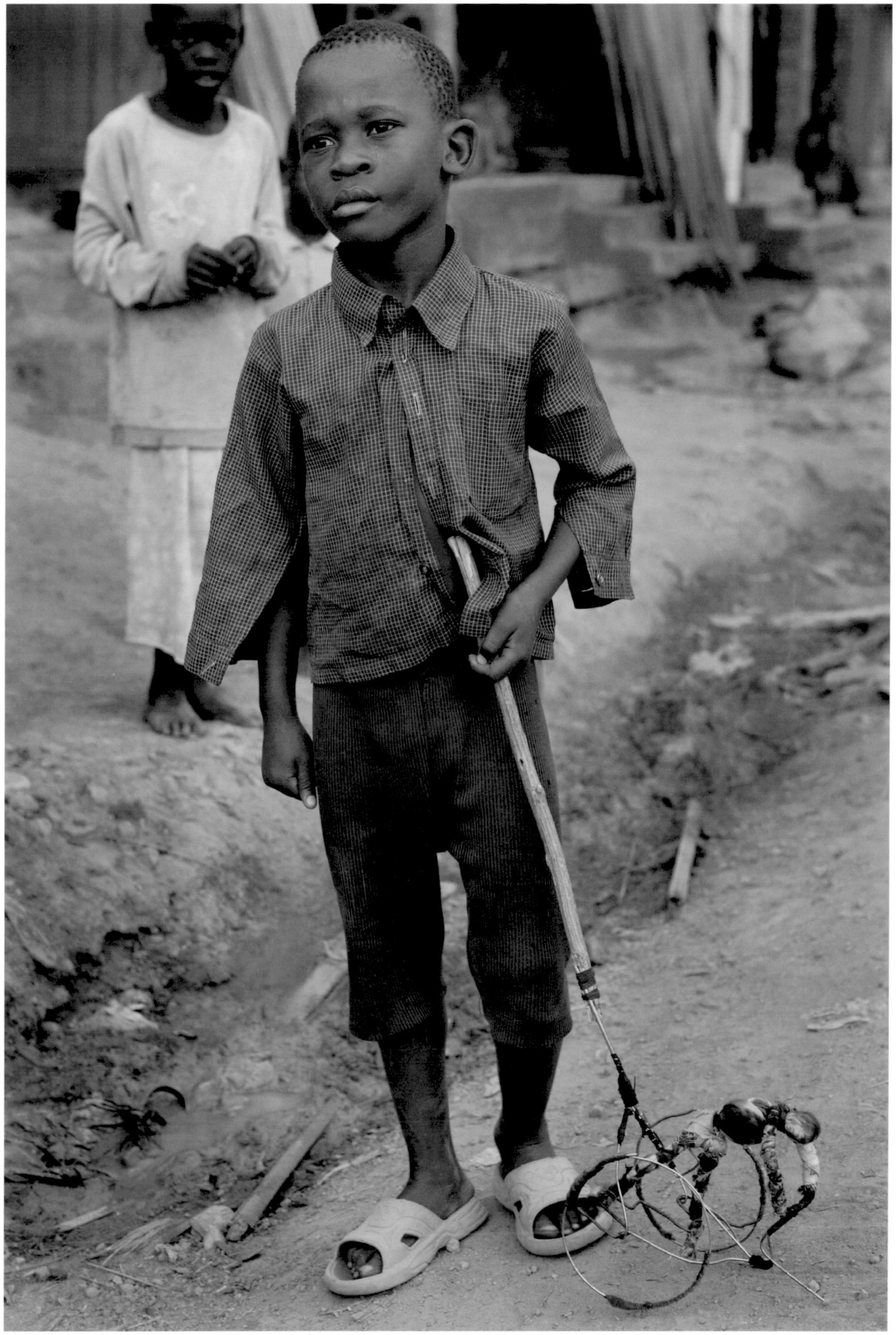

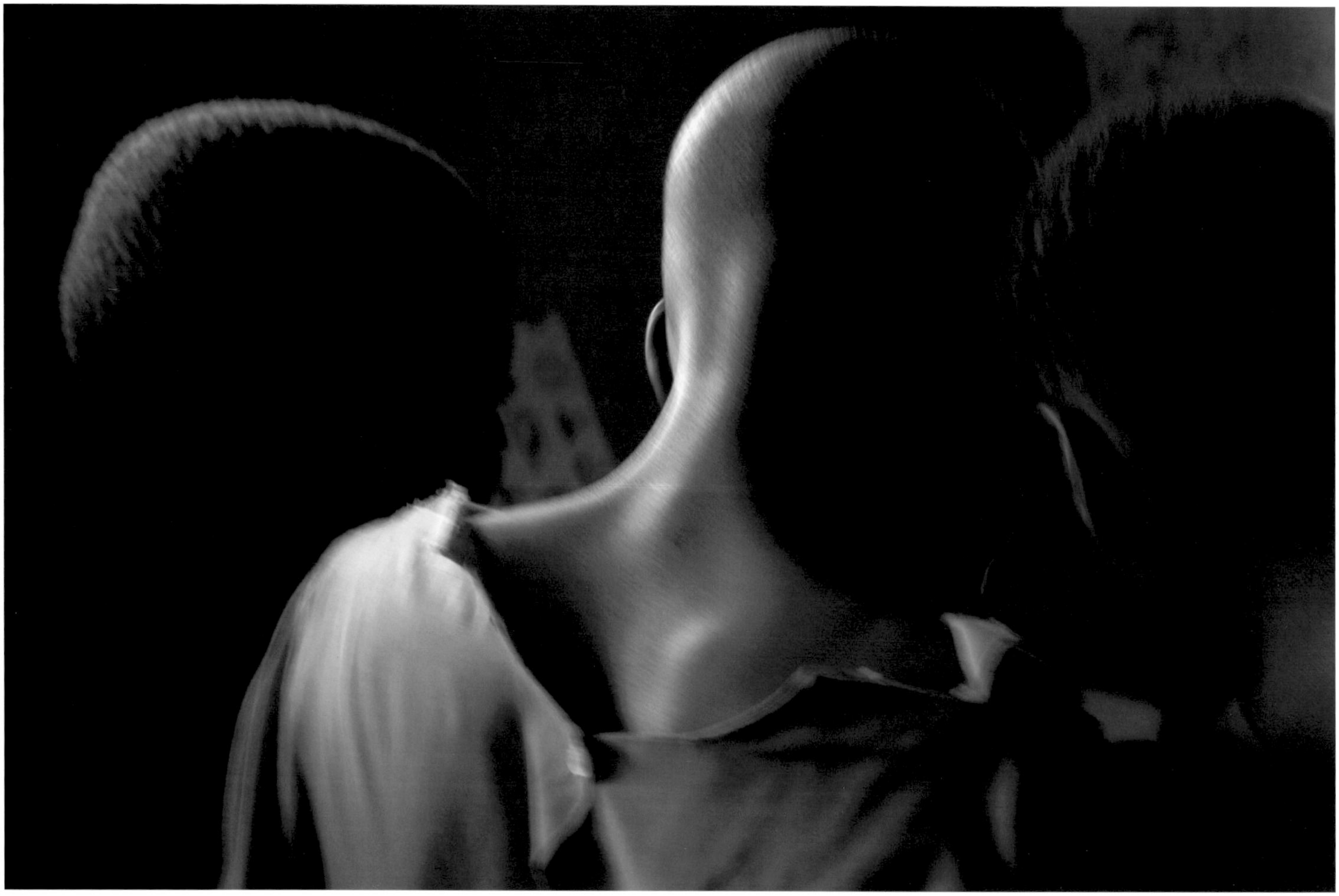

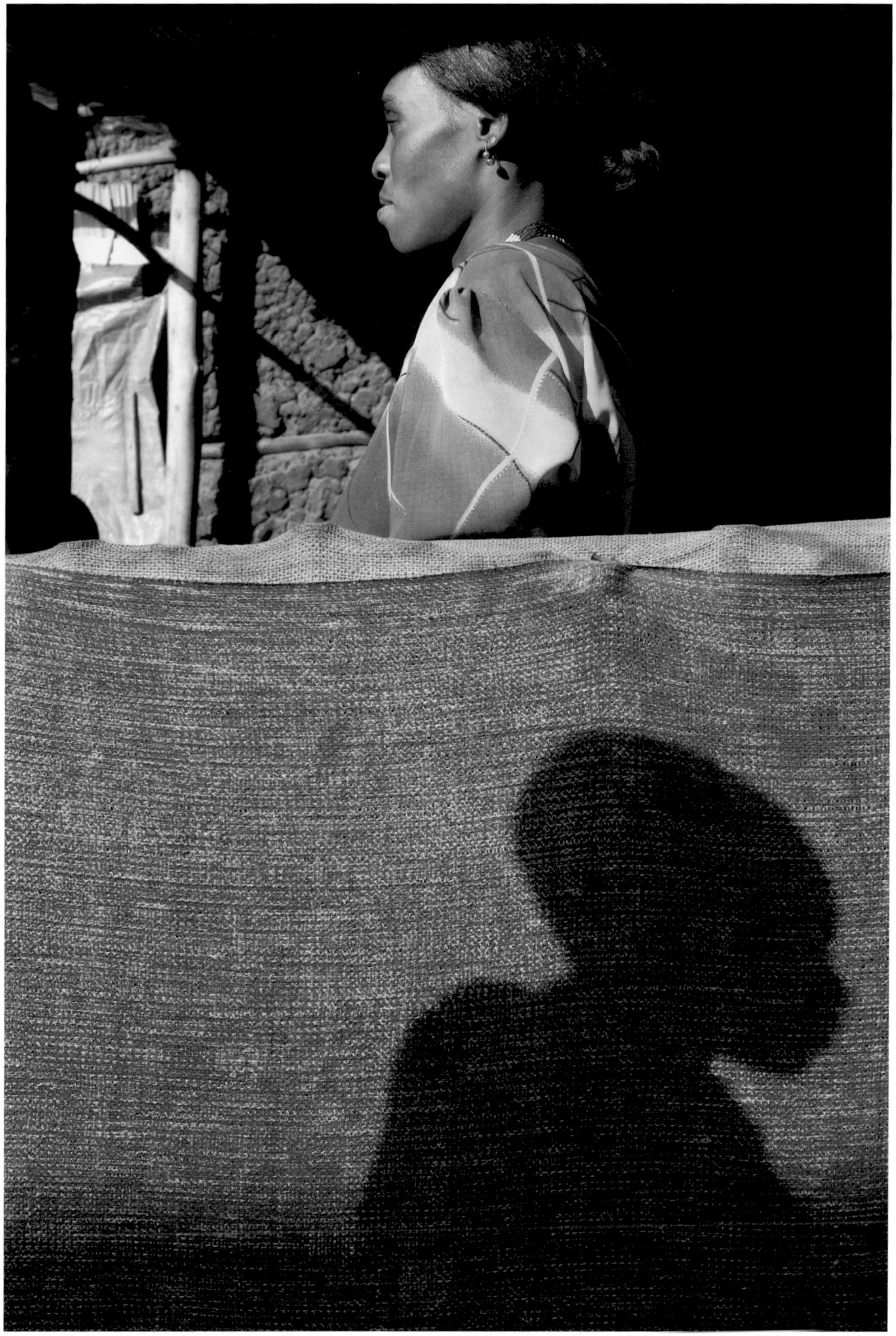

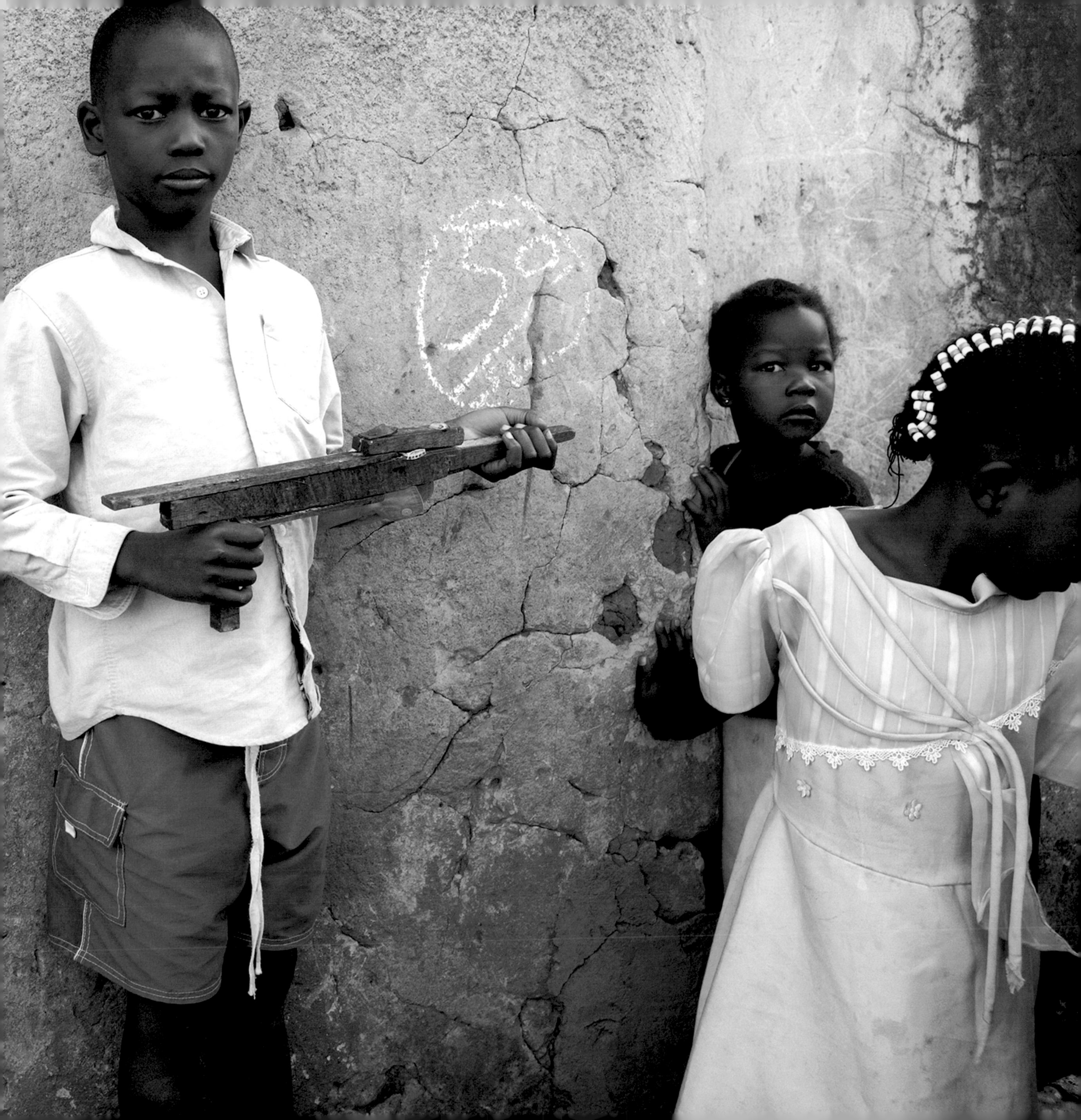

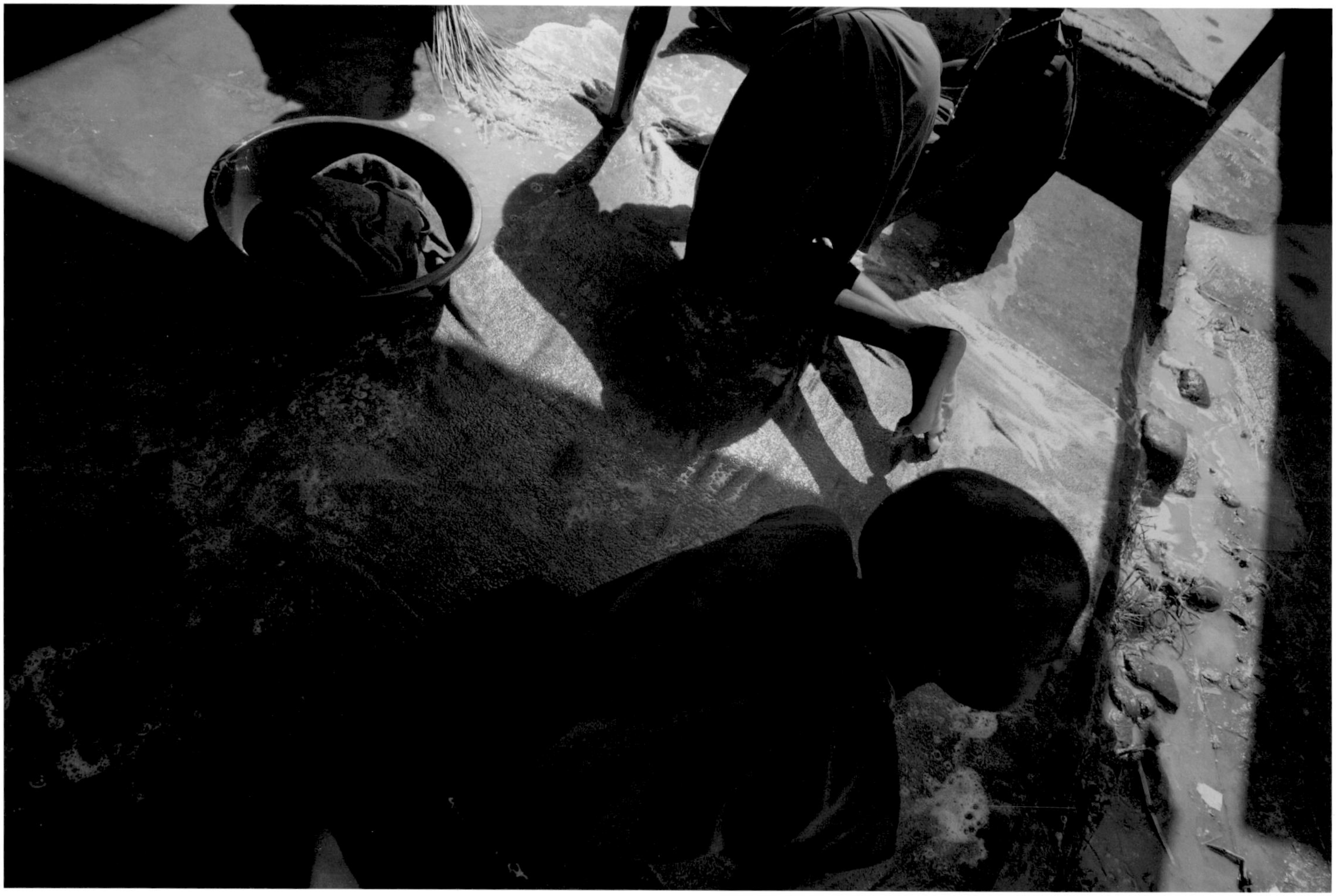

contrast

+ page
atten

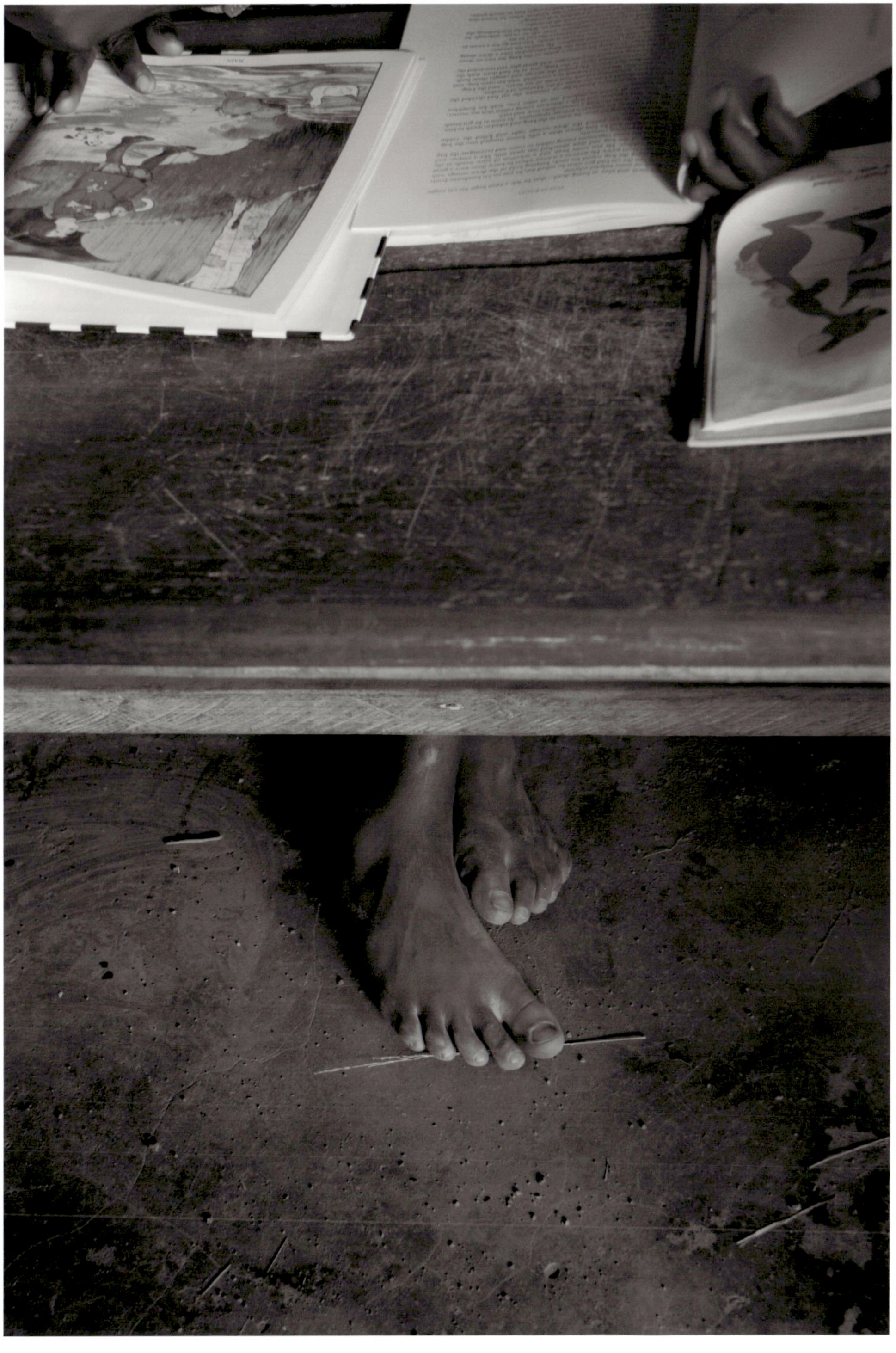

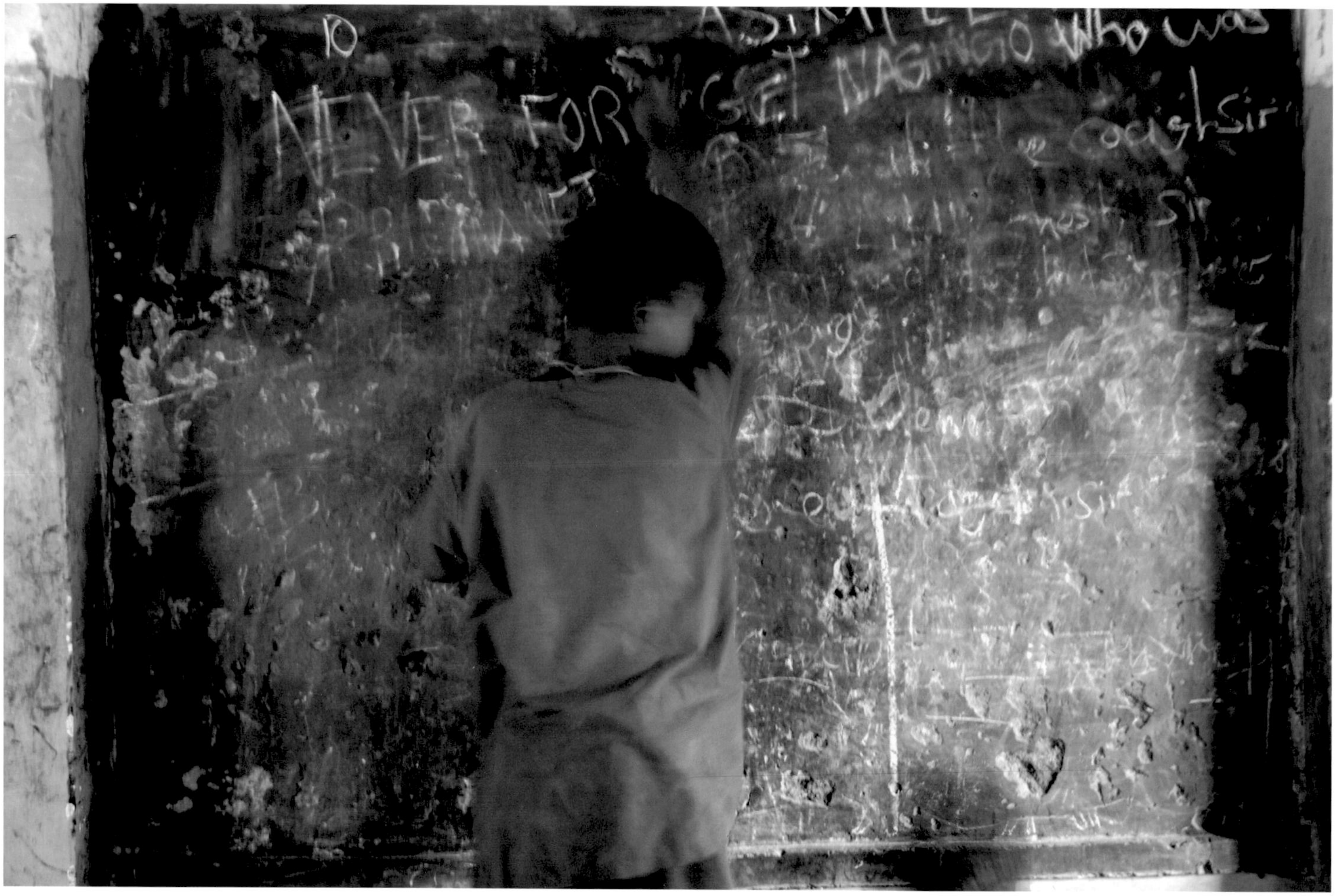
NEVER FOR GET
who was

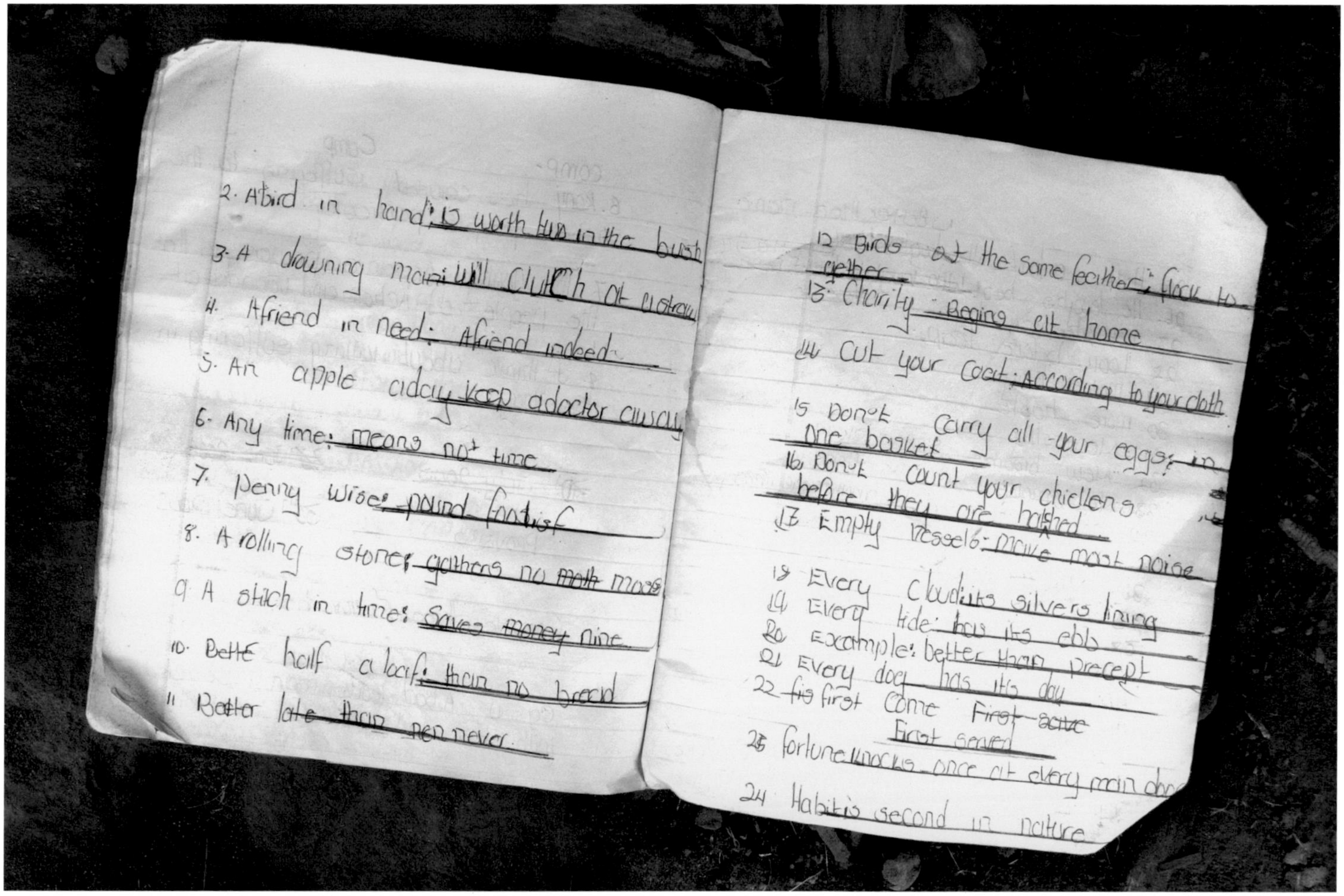
2. A bird in hand: is worth two in the bush
3. A drowning man: will clutch at a straw
4. A friend in need: A friend indeed.
5. An apple a day keep a doctor away
6. Any time: means no time
7. Penny wise: pound foolish
8. A rolling stone: gathers no moss
9 A stich in time: Saves nine
10. Better half a loaf: than no bread
11 Better late than never.
12 Birds of the same feather: flock together
13 Charity: Begins at home
14 Cut your coat: according to your cloth
15 Don't carry all your eggs: in one basket
16 Don't count your chickens before they are hatched
17 Empty vessels: make most noise
18 Every cloud: its silvers lining
19 Every tide: has its ebb
20 Example: better than precept
21 Every dog has its day
22 first come First served
23 fortune knocks once at every man door
24 Habit is second in nature

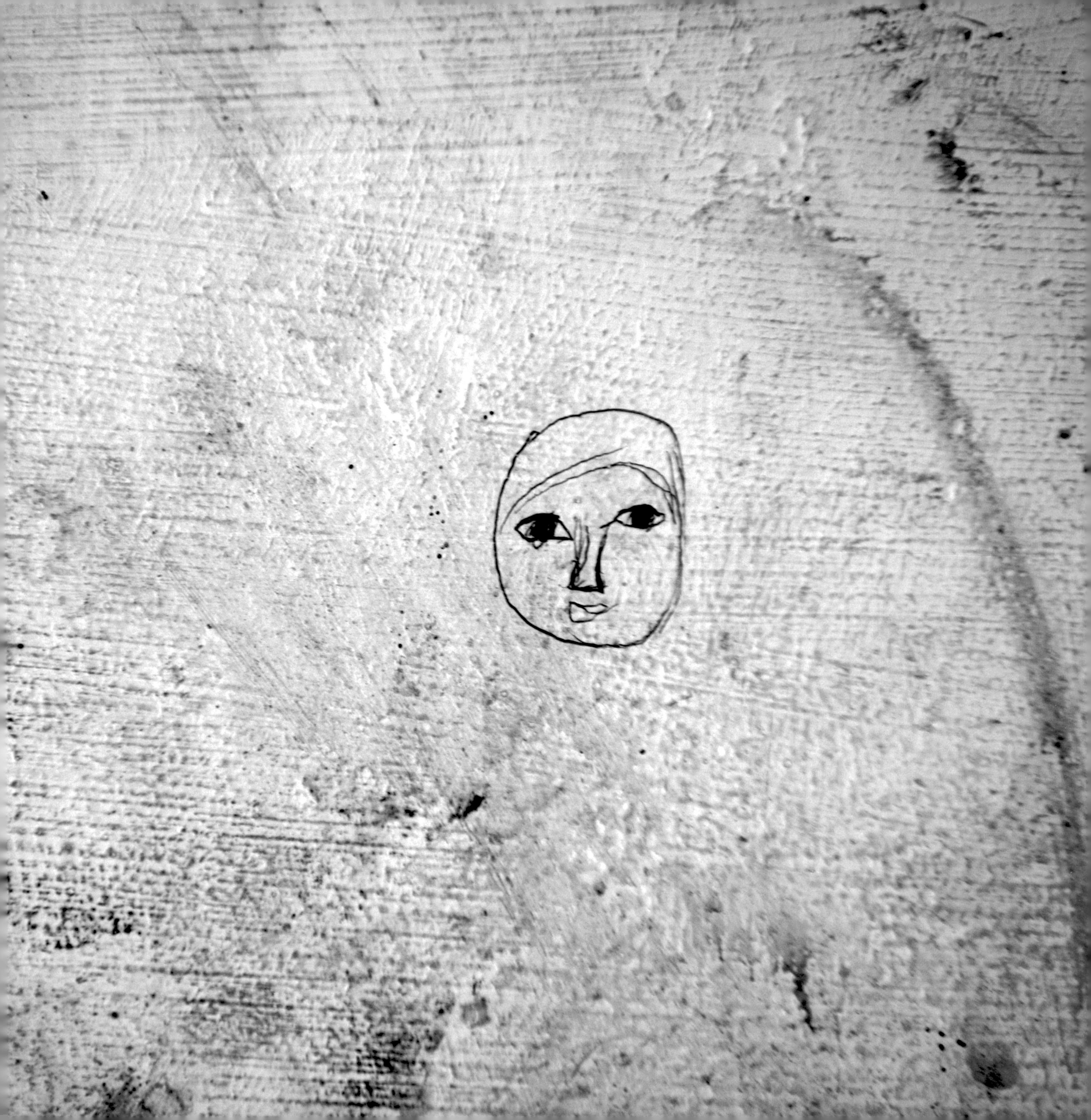

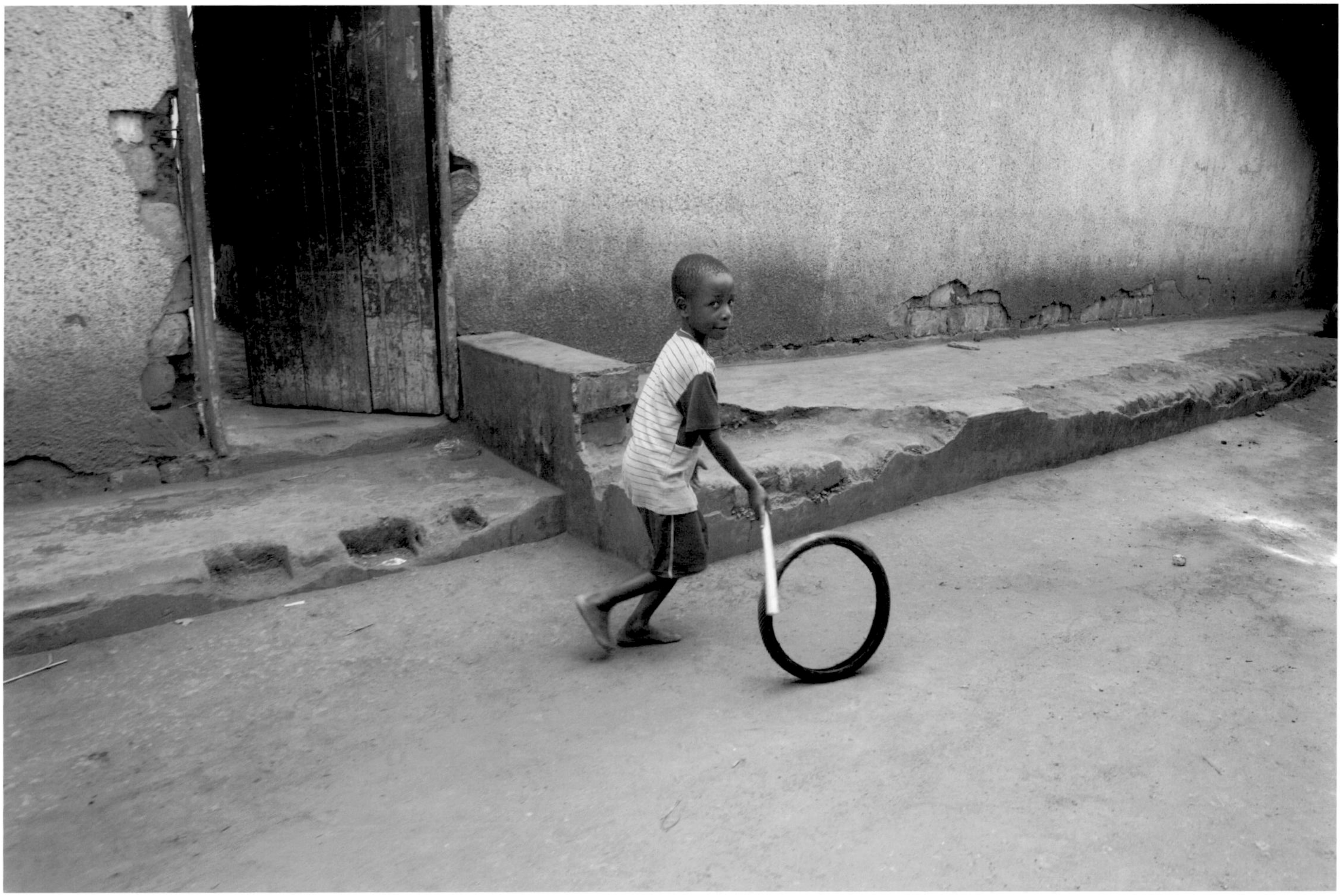

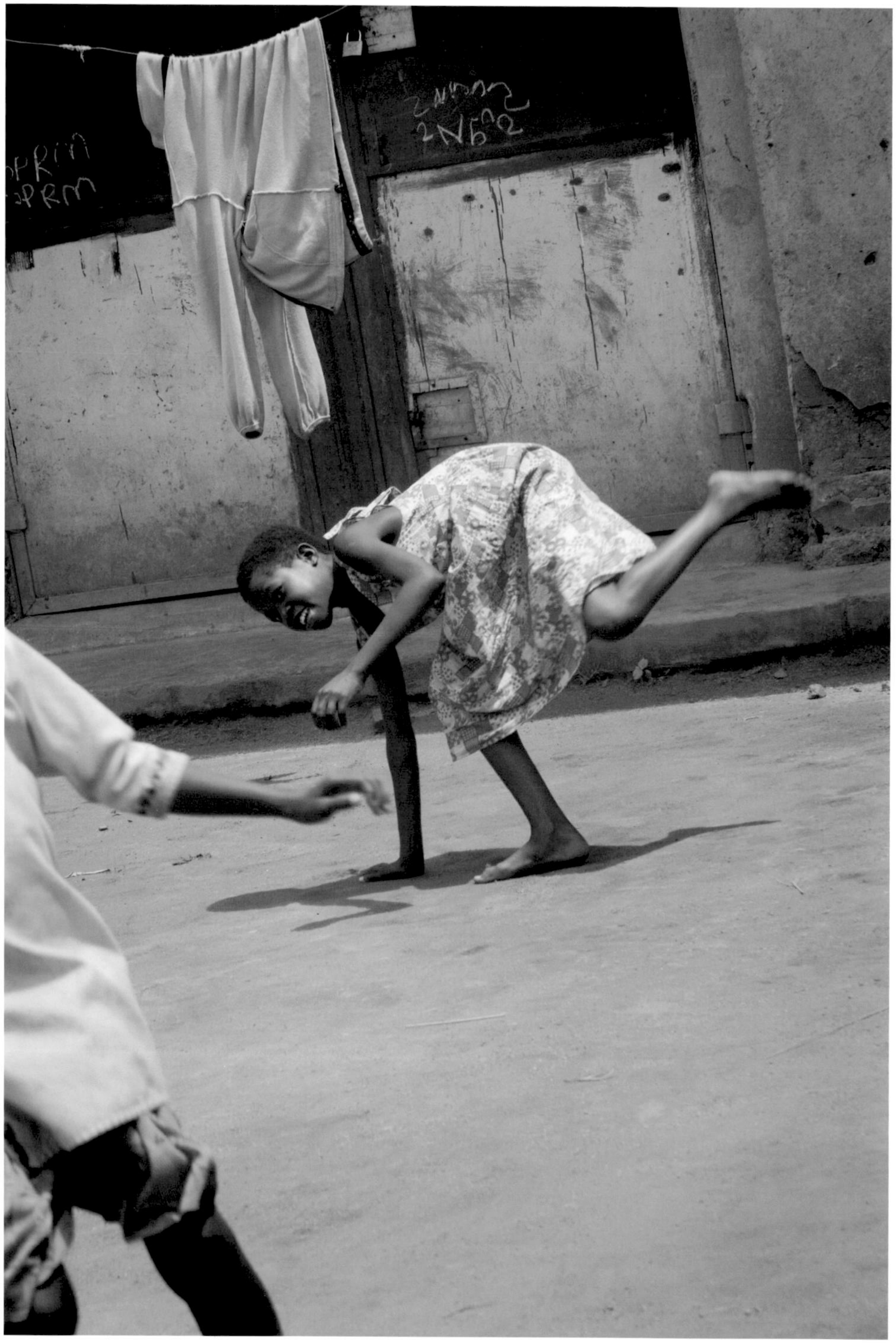

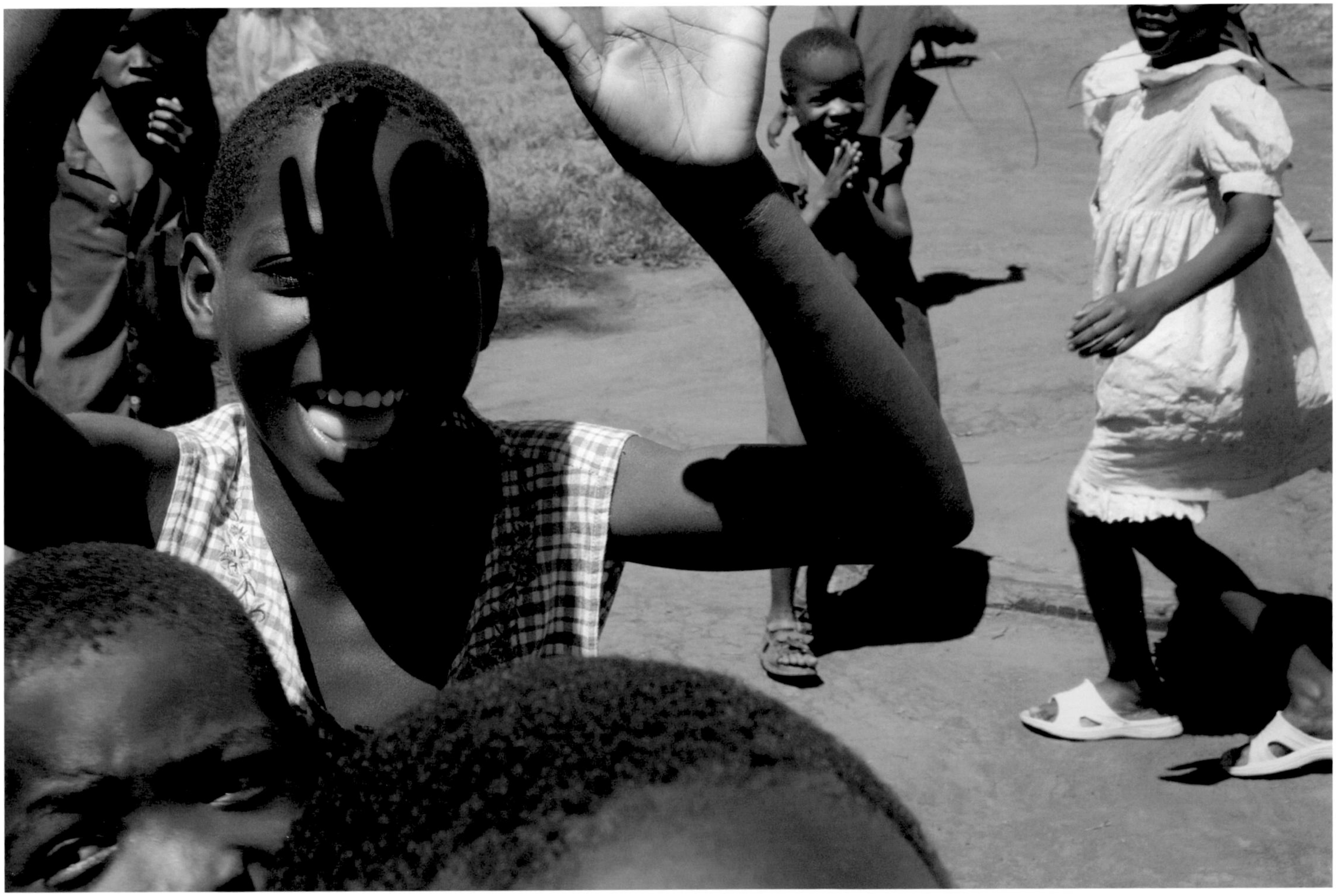

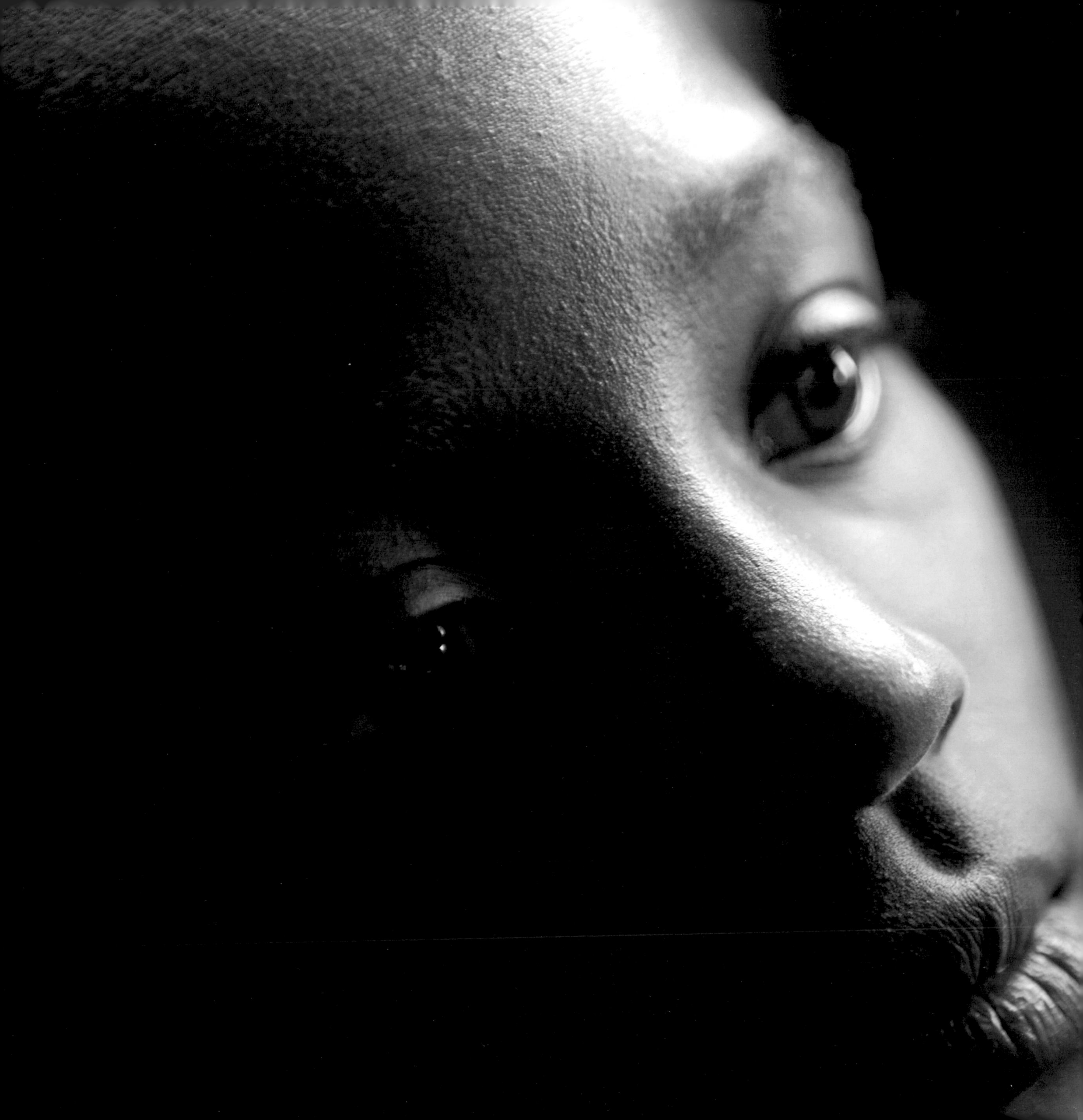

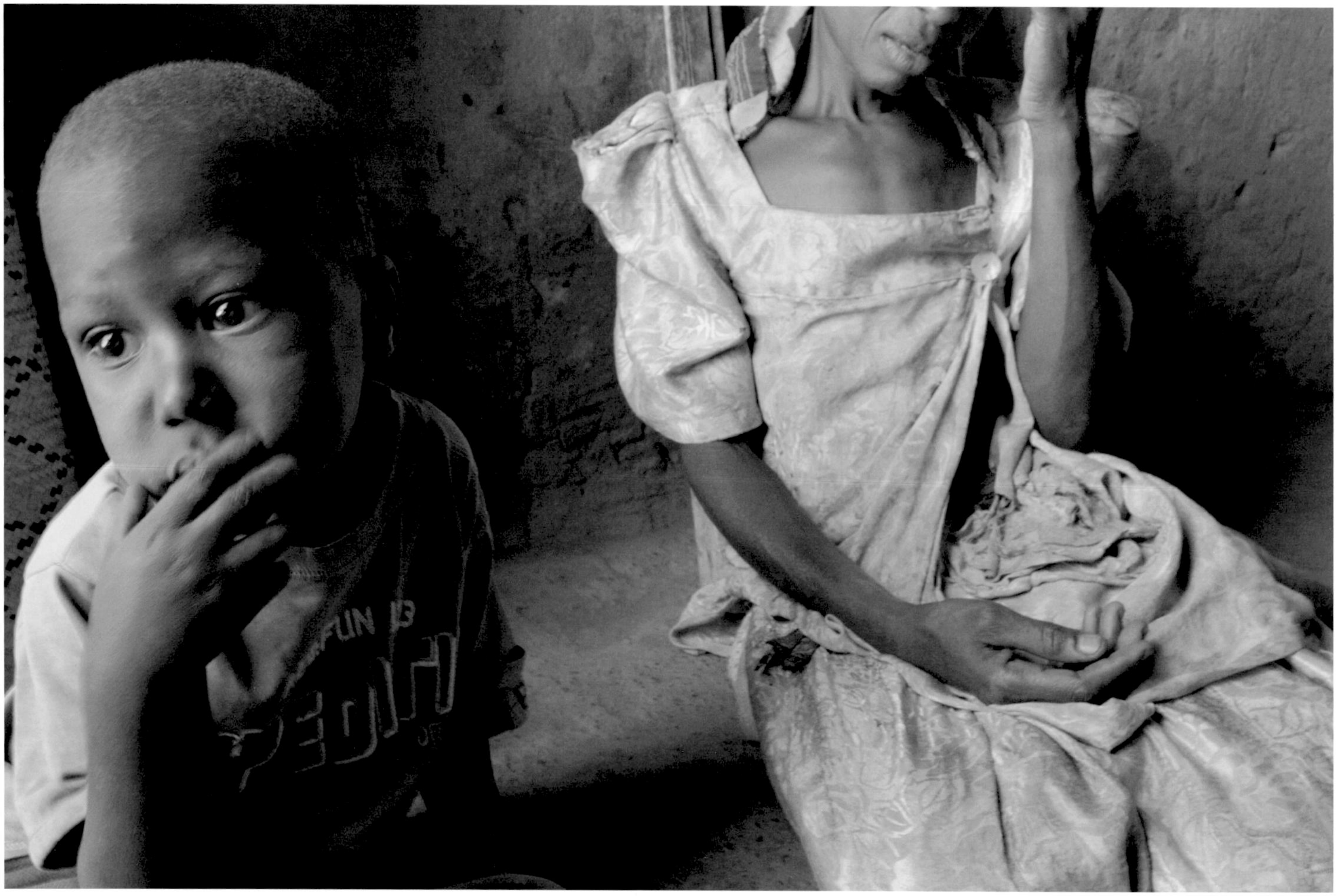

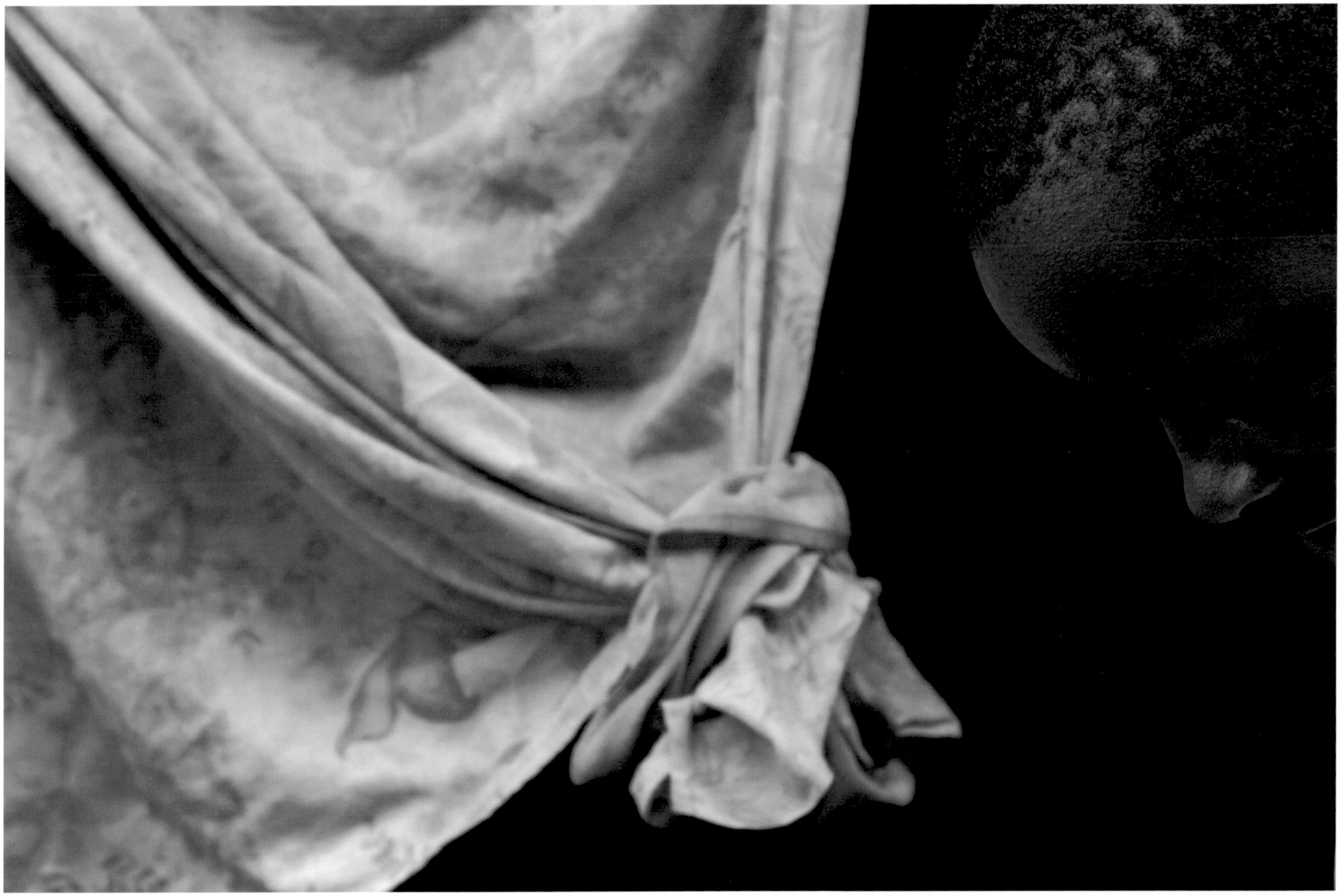

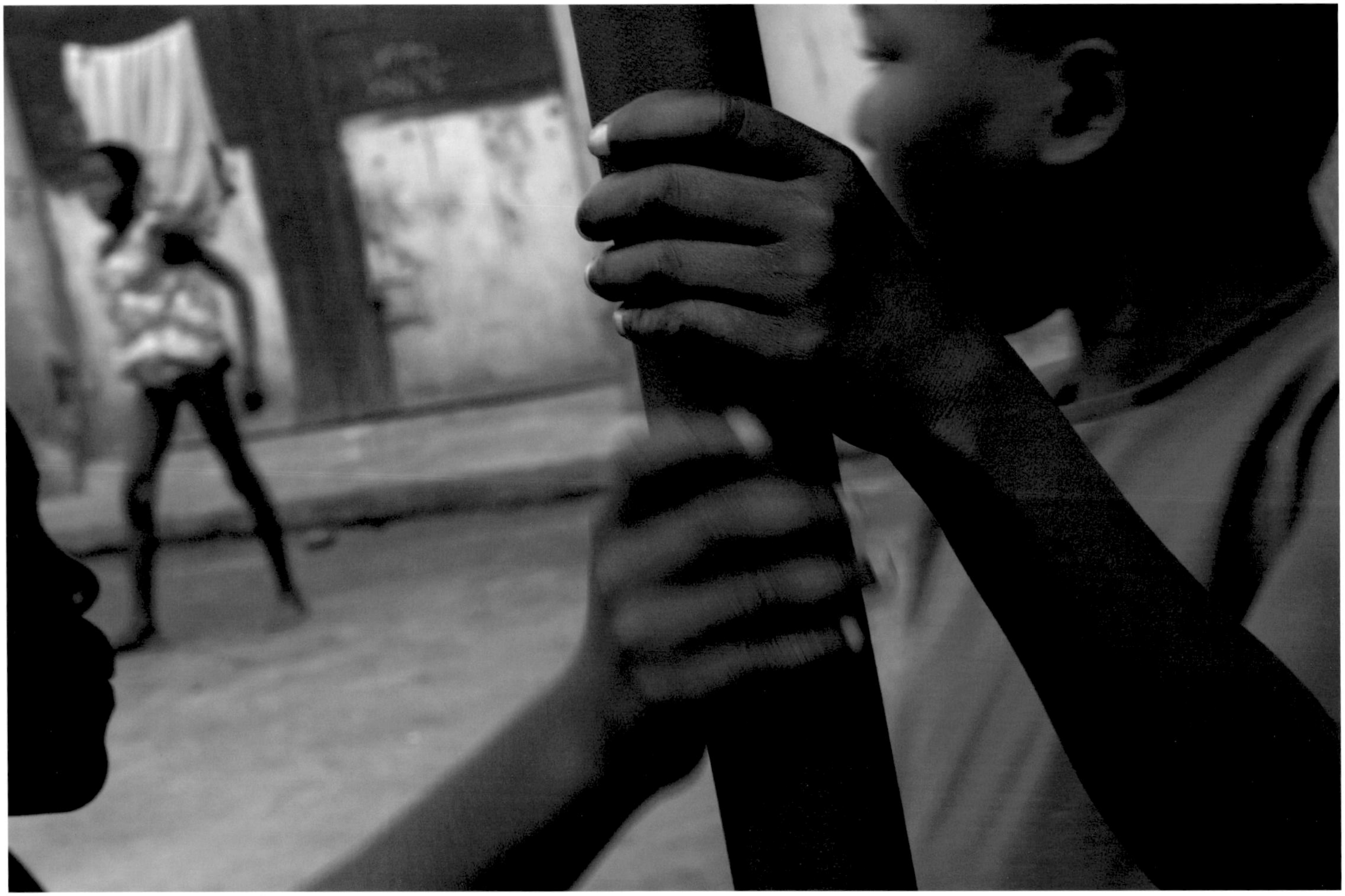

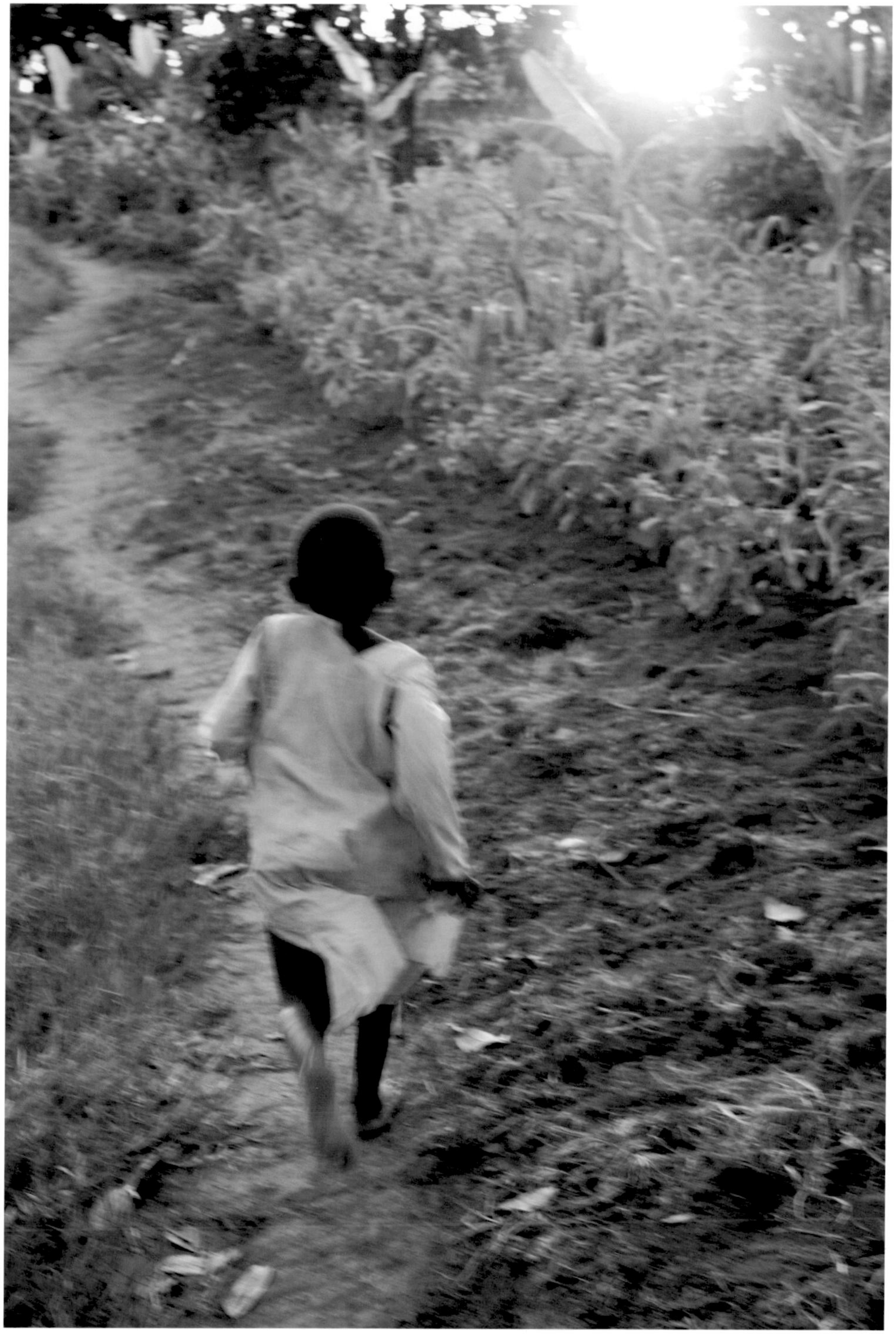

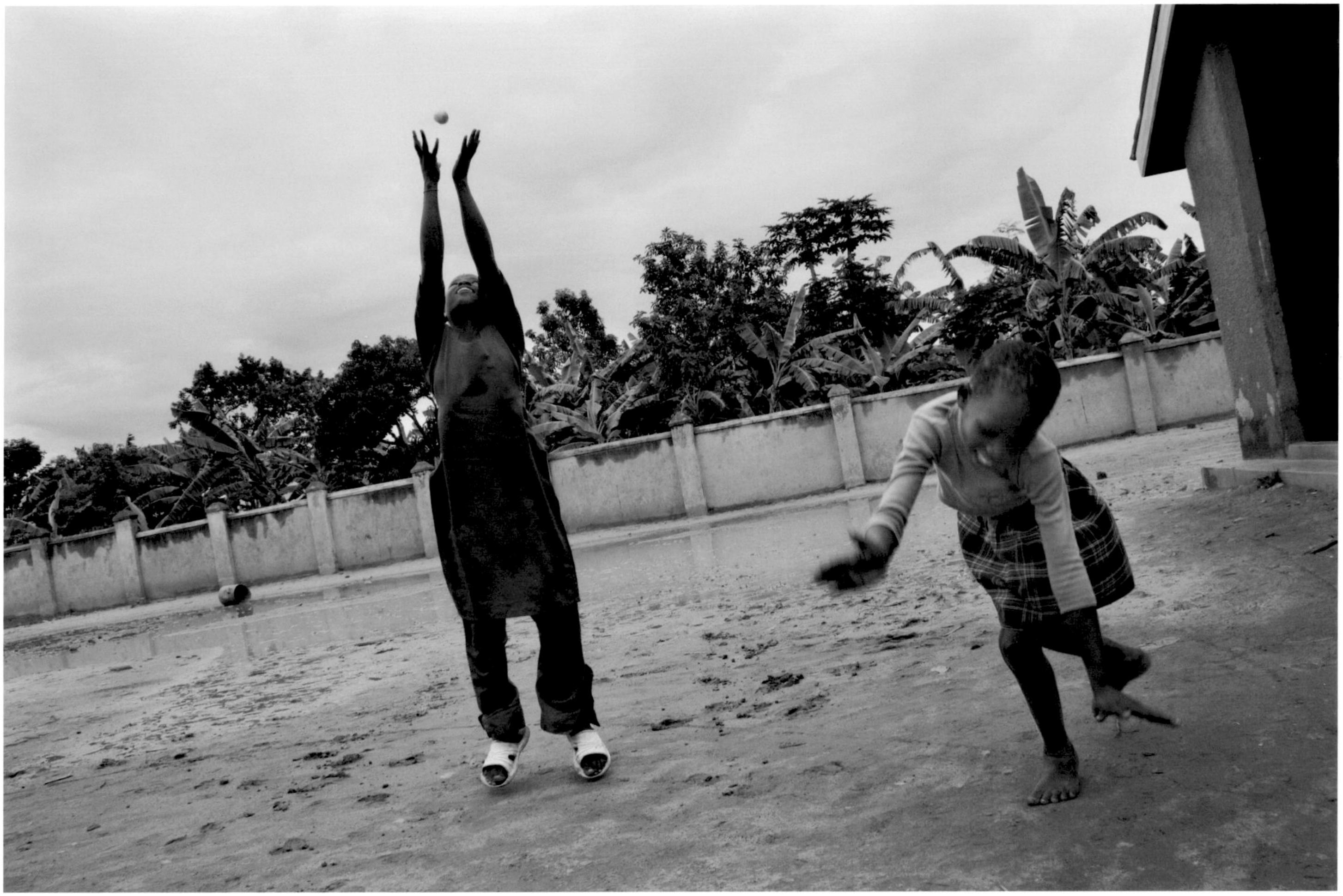

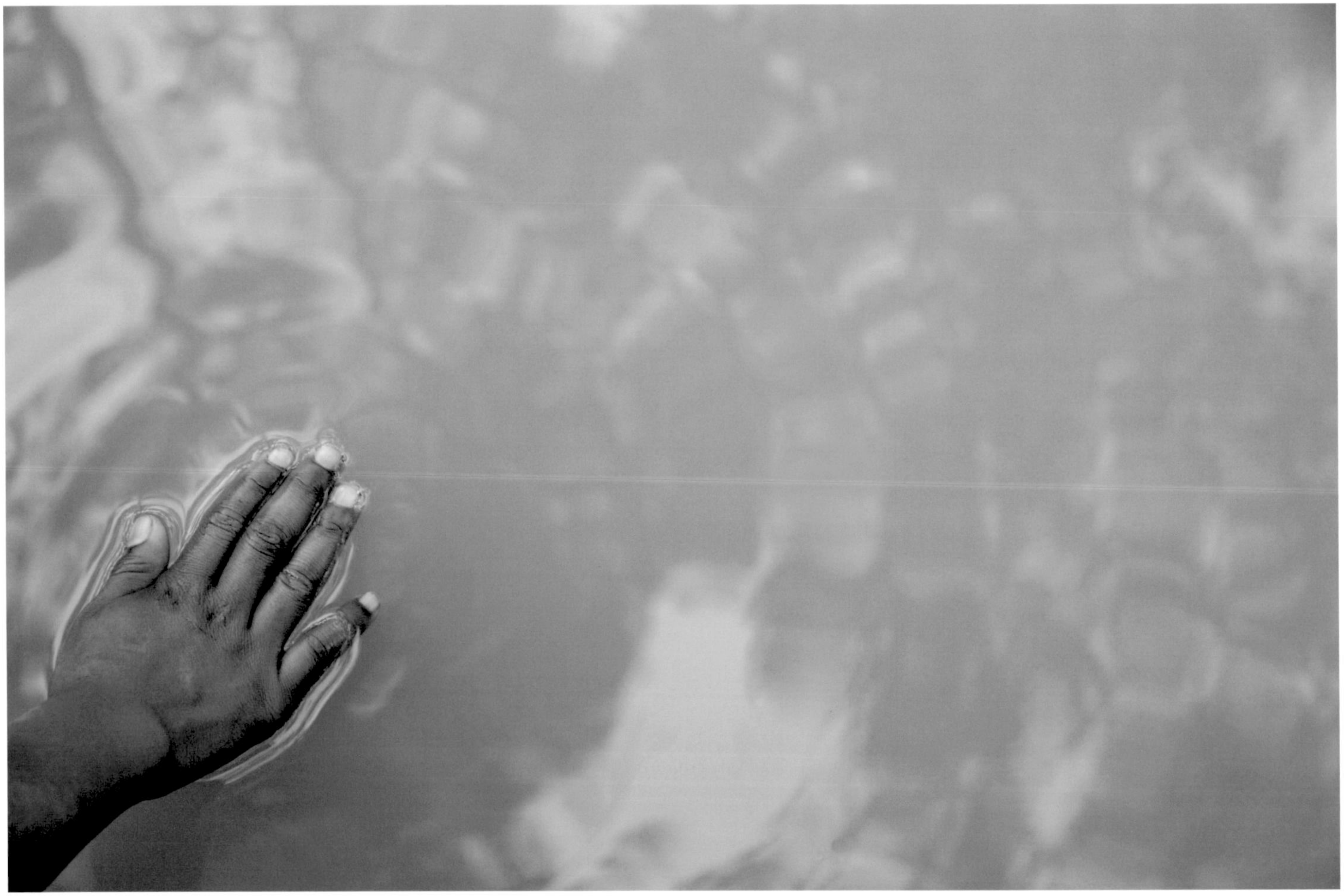

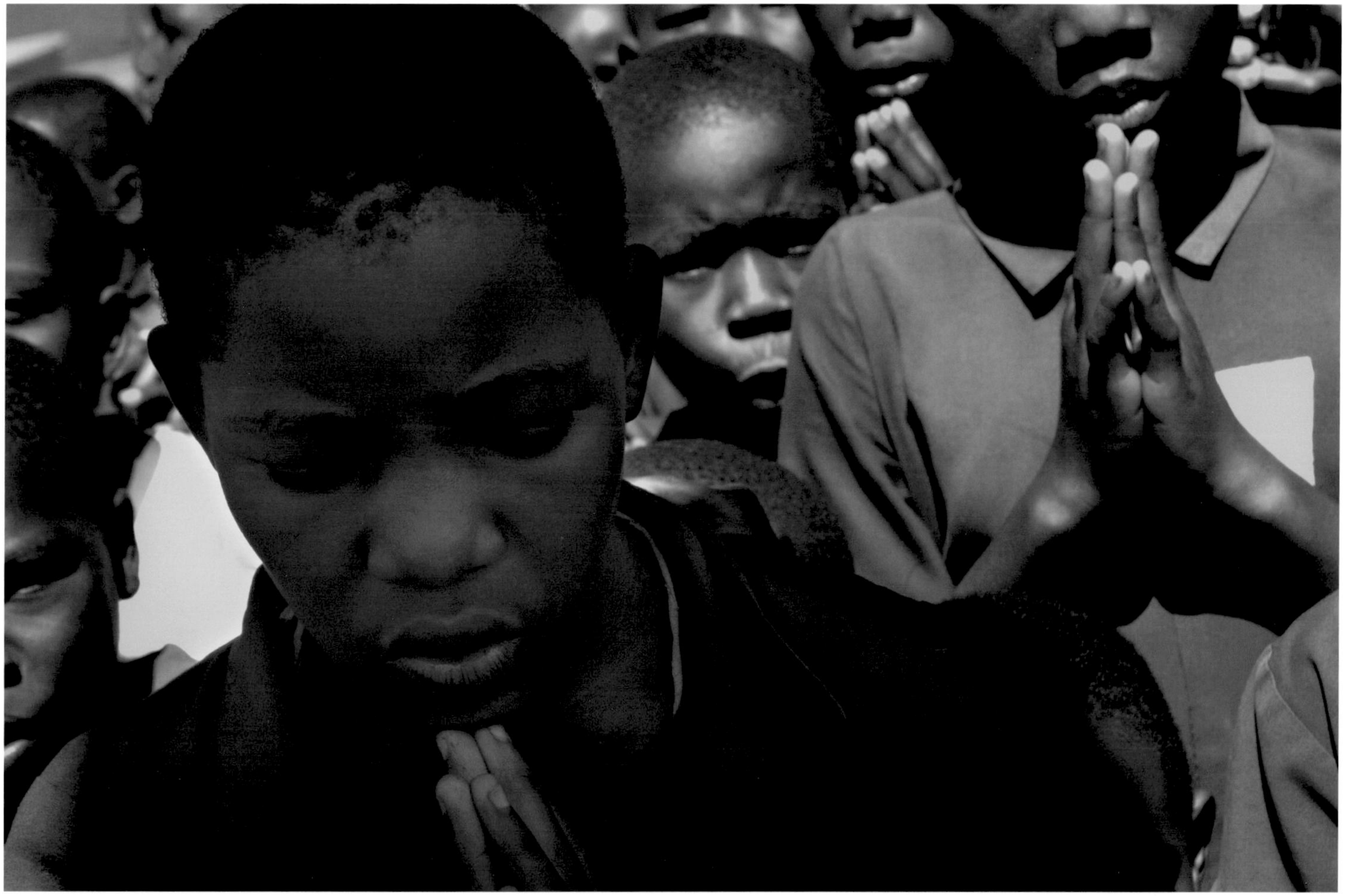

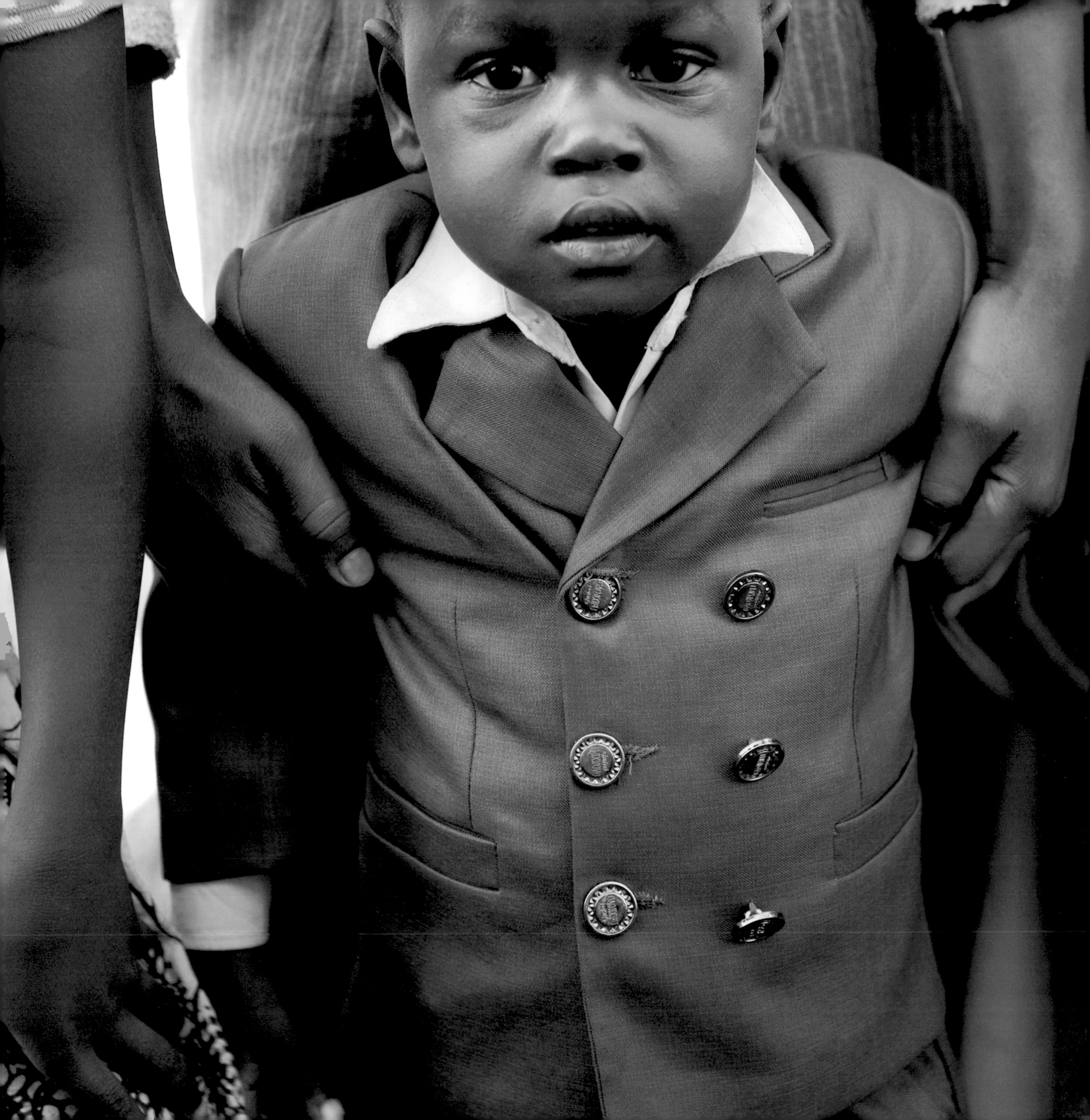

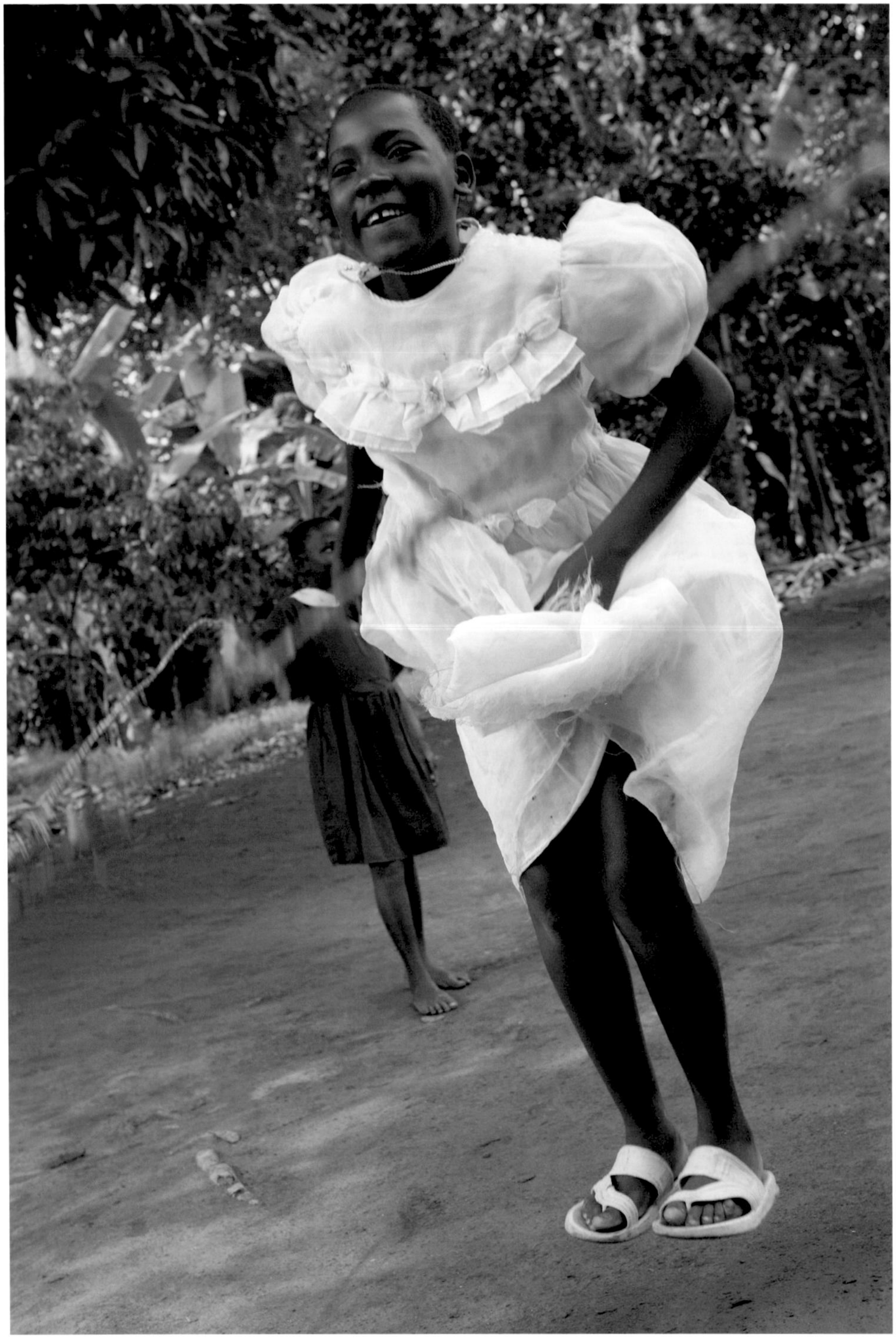

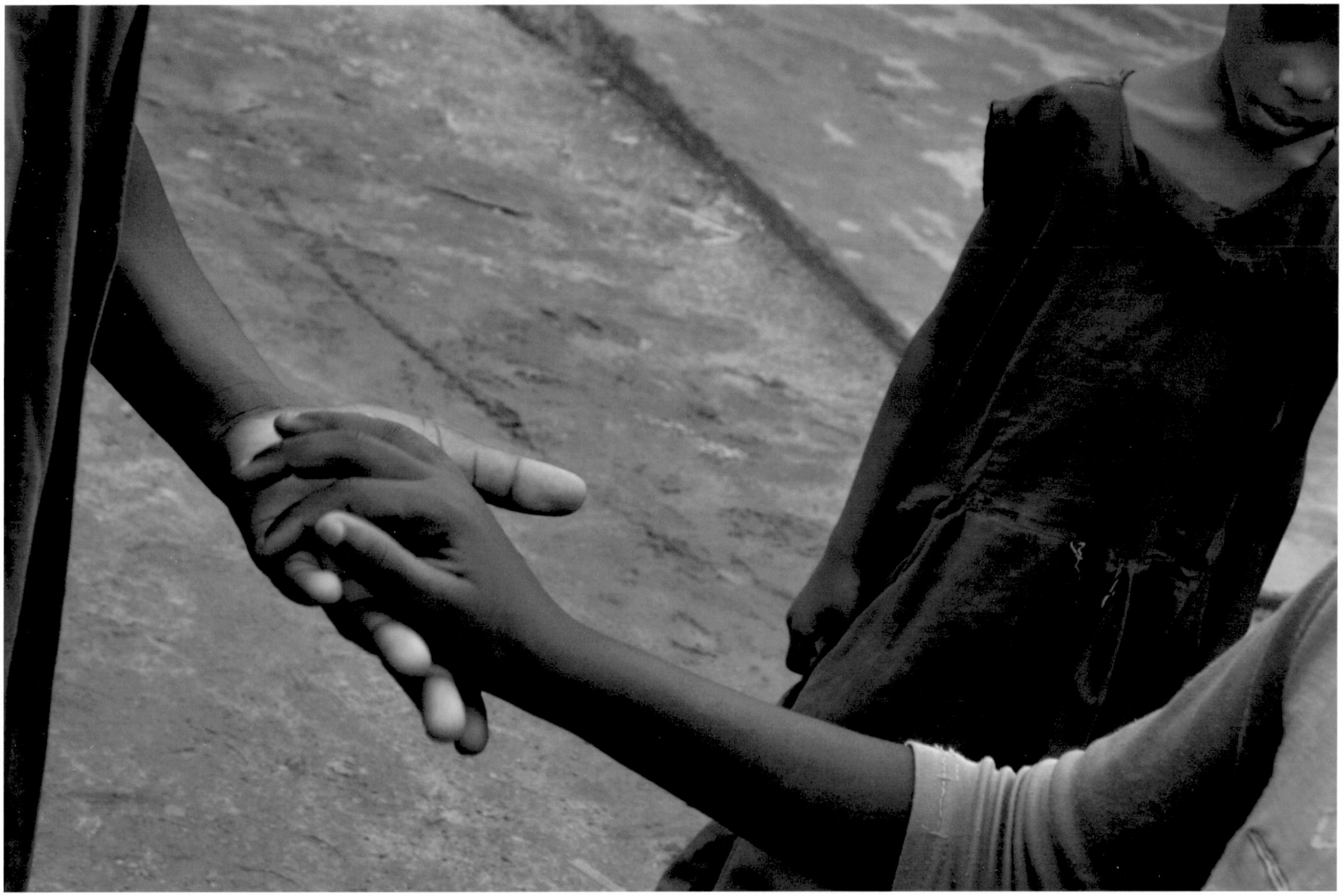

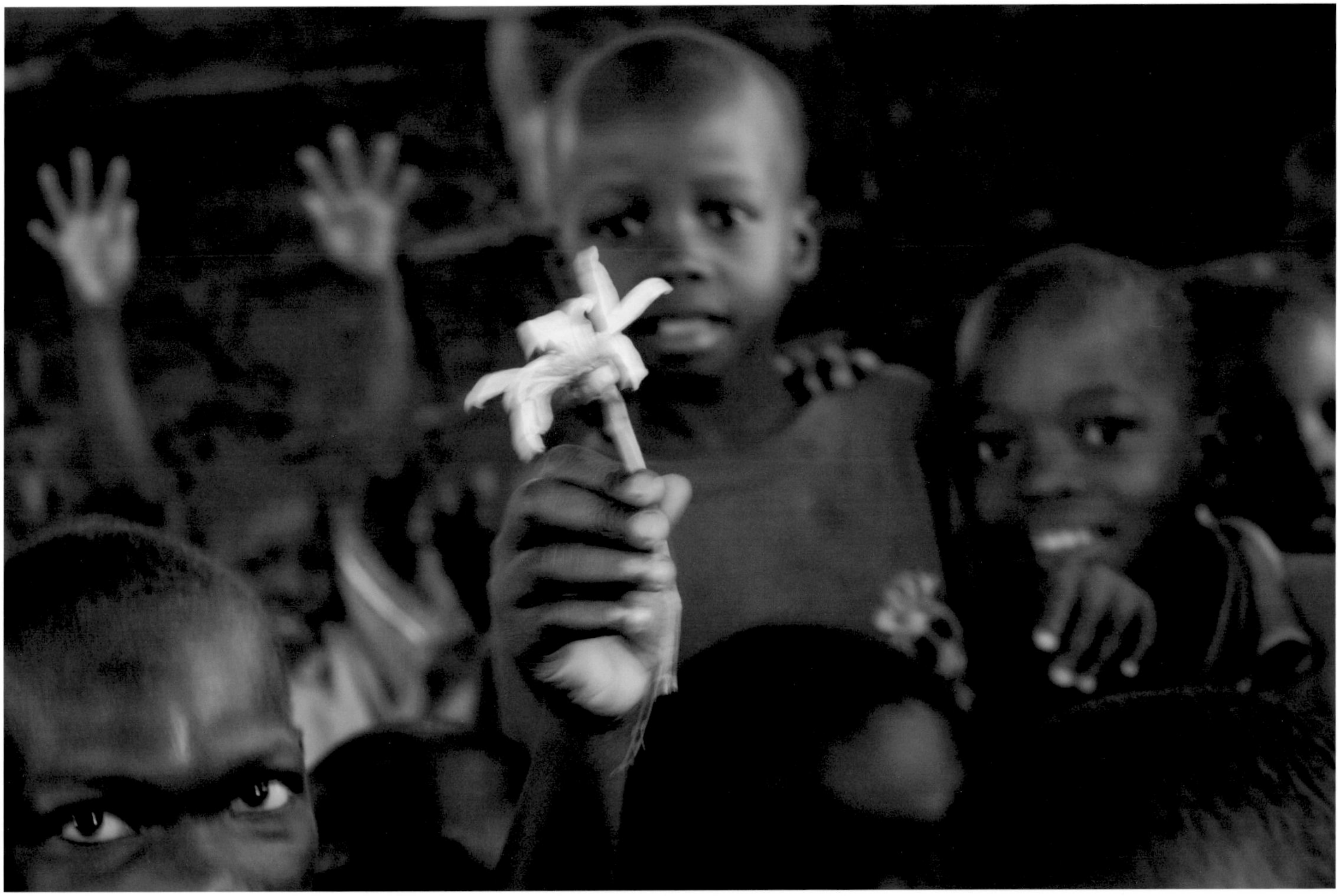

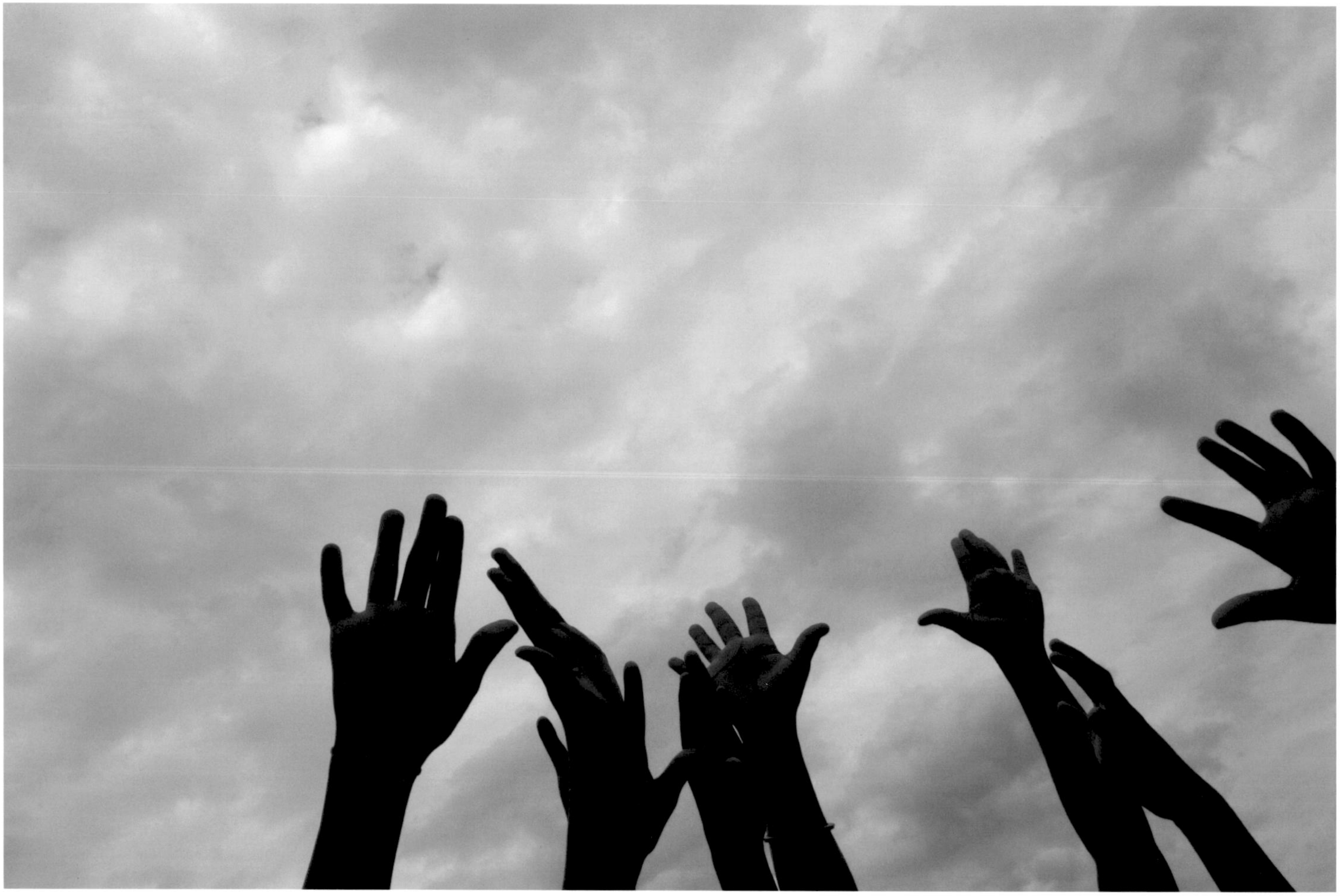

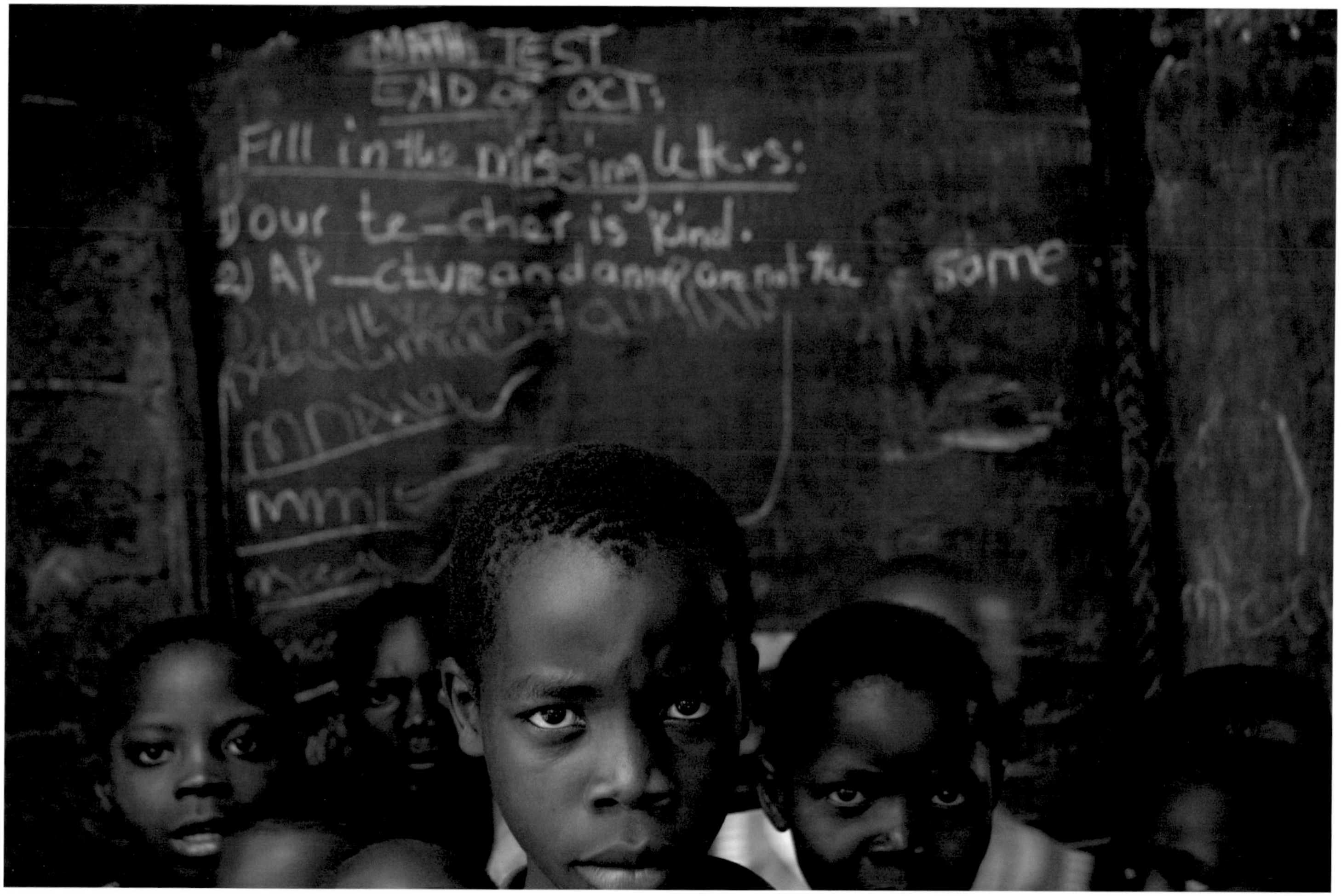
TEST
Fill in the missing letters:
our te_cher is kind.
same

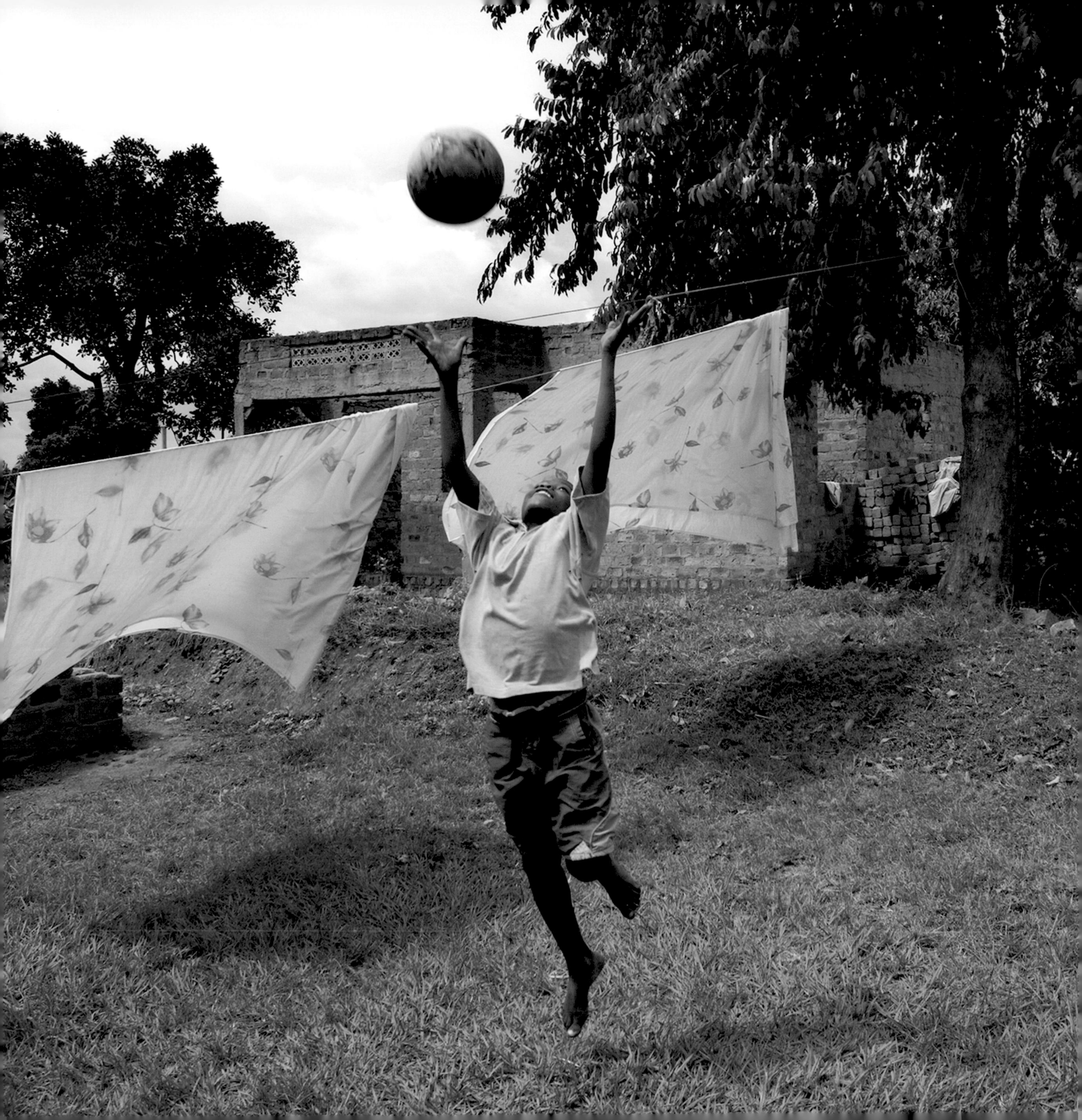

YITAMU

(reach through)

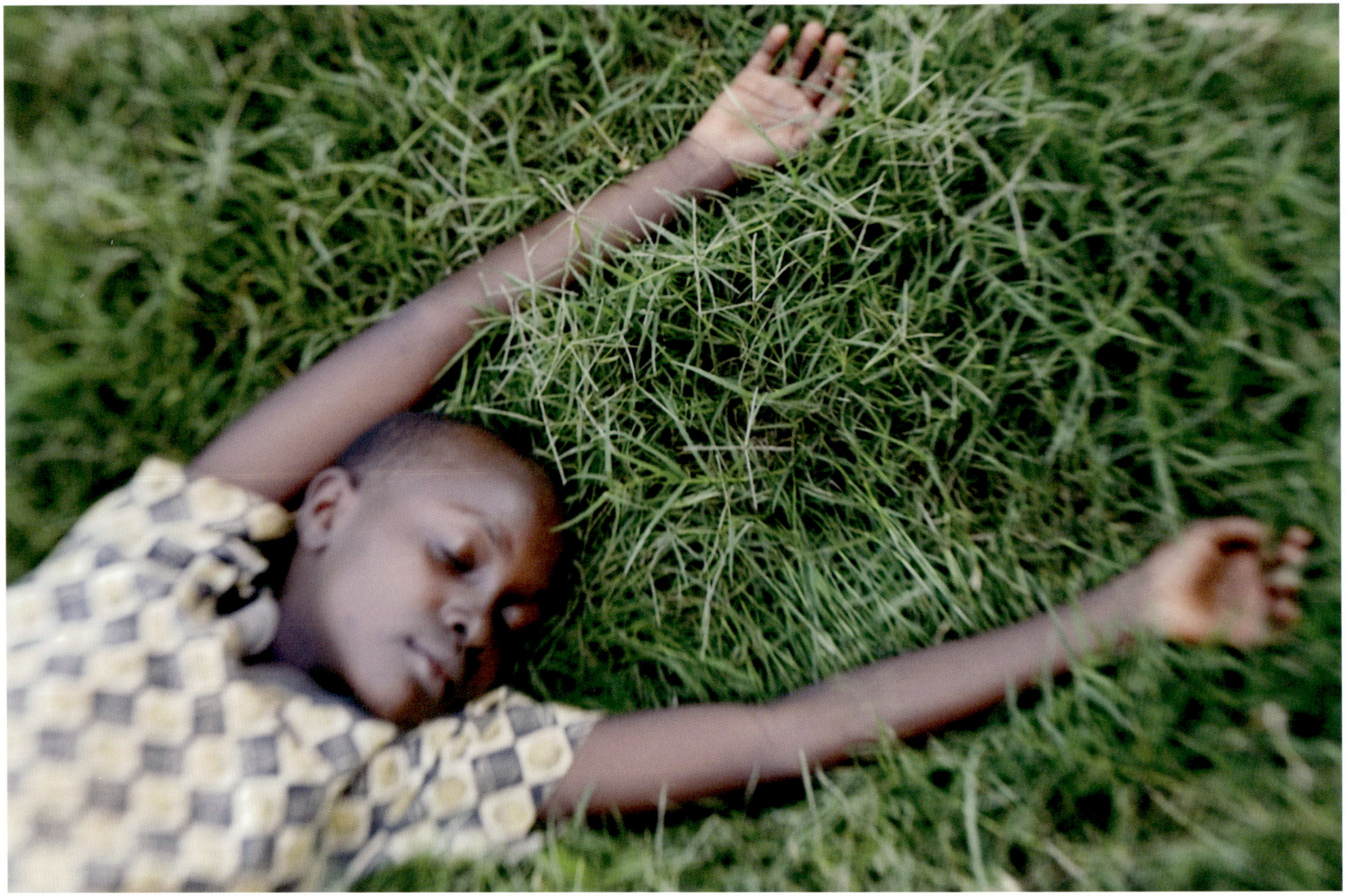

ISABELLA, AGE 11

Sometimes I dream that the ground is breaking
and I am falling down in there. When I wake up,
I think it is true and I cry.

CALEB, AGE 11

When I was asleep, I dreamed that I was with my mum at home,
and an Englishman came to our home. He took me to England to play football.
When we reached there, I started playing, and I sent my mum money.

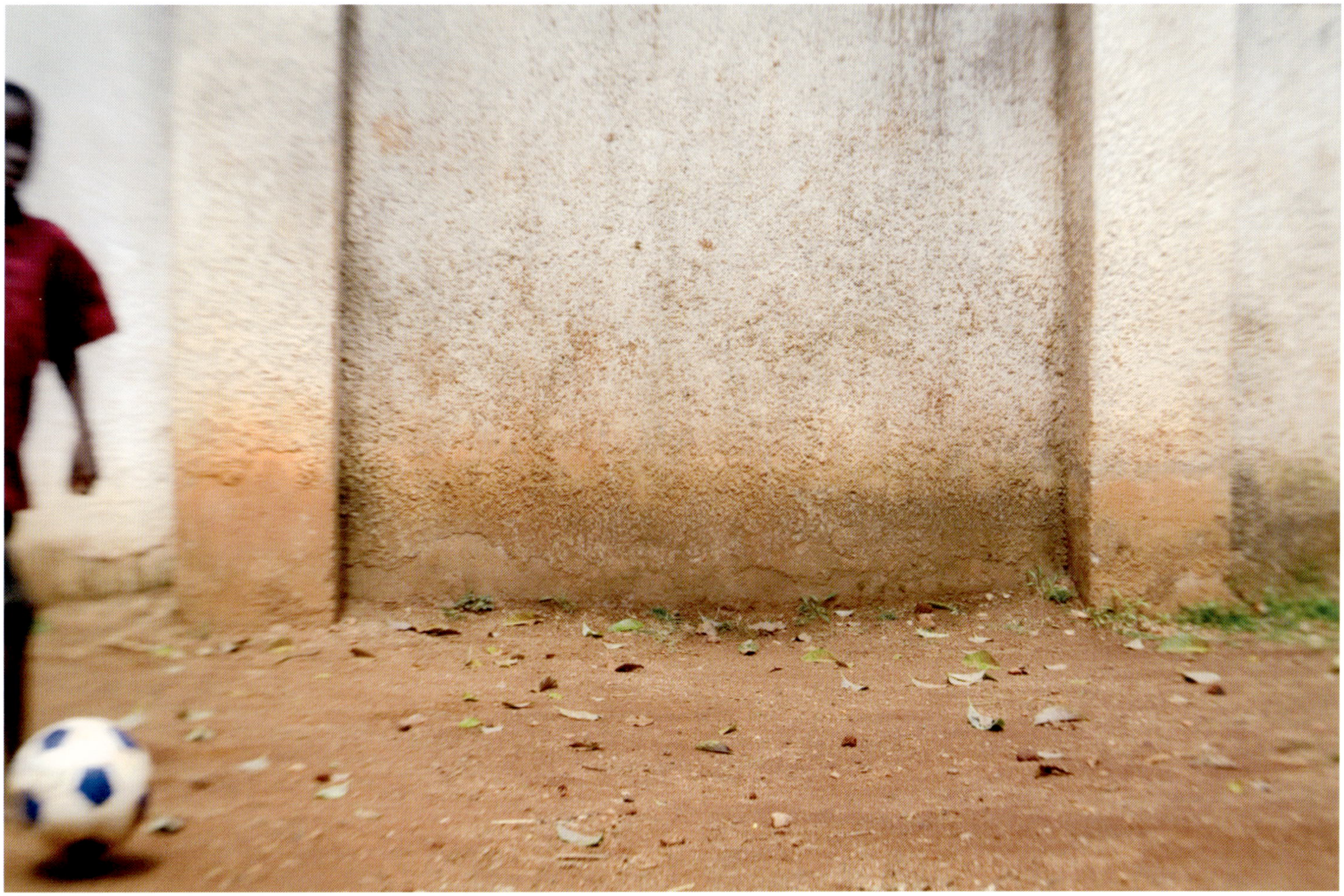

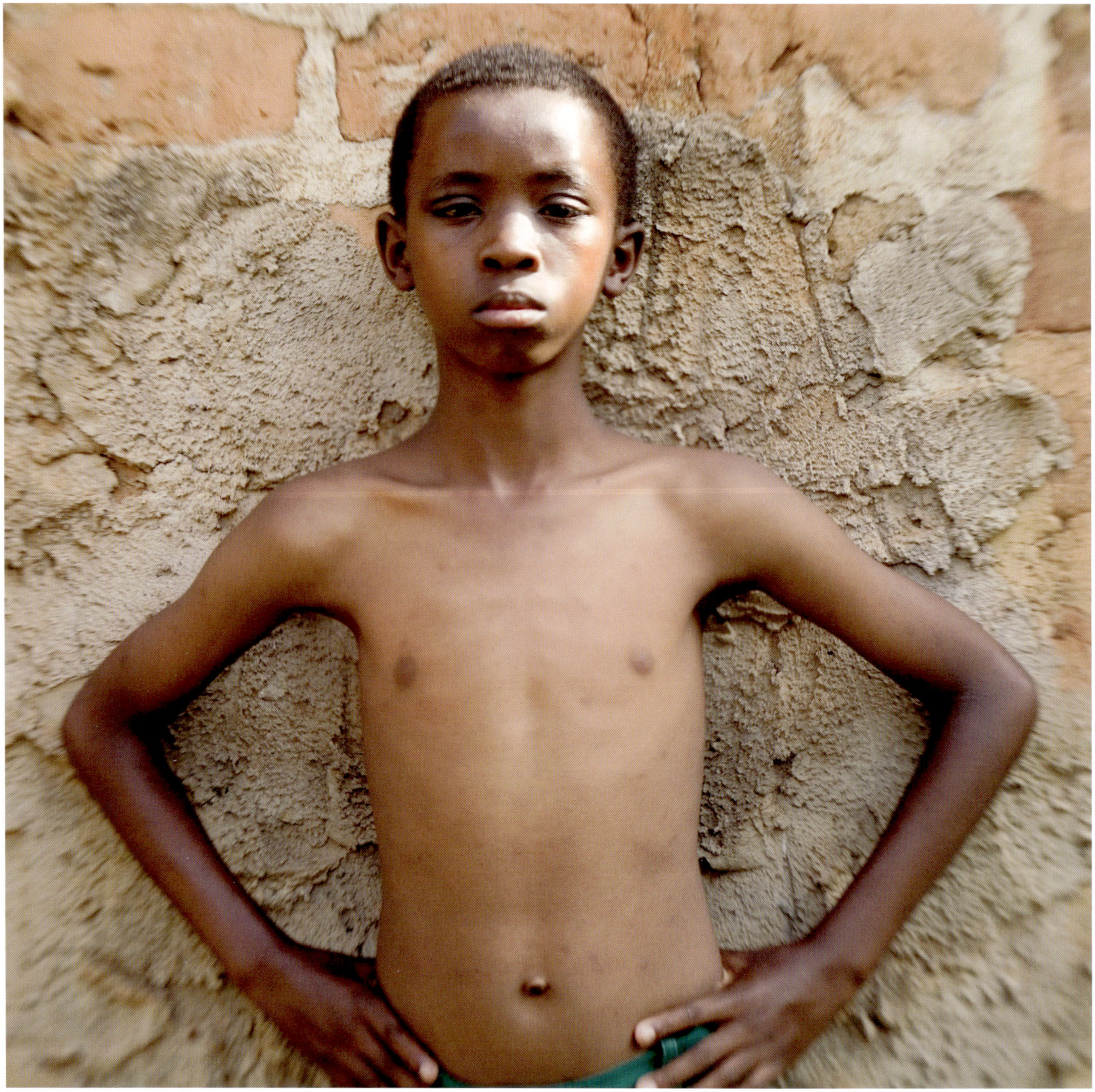

JULIUS, AGE 11

I got a dream that I was grown up and I was a boss, and I was rich.

MACKLINE, AGE 10

I walked to our village. It was very far.
There my mum was going to the garden and she saw a big snake.
She killed the big snake. The mother of the snake wanted to kill my mother
because she had killed its child.

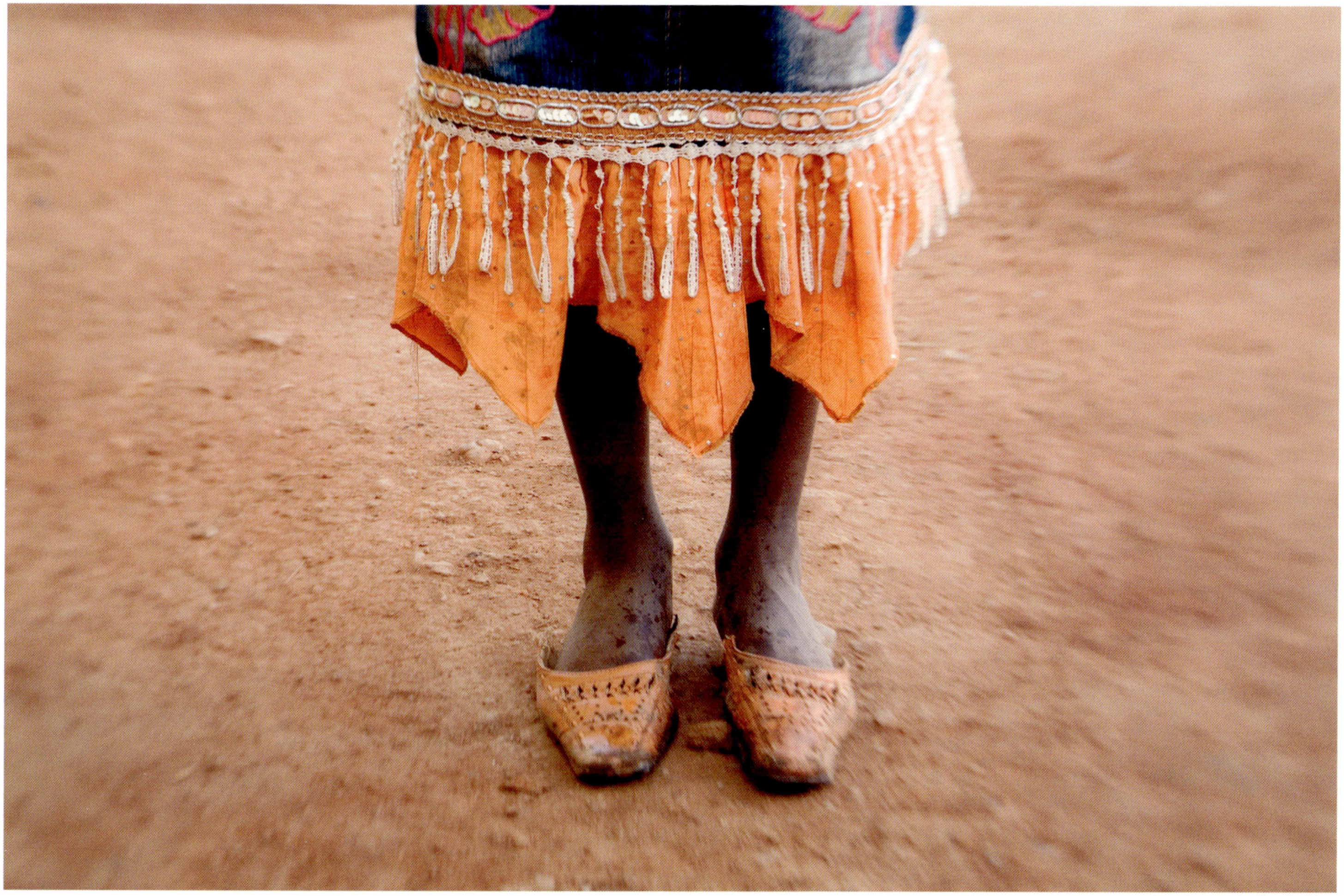

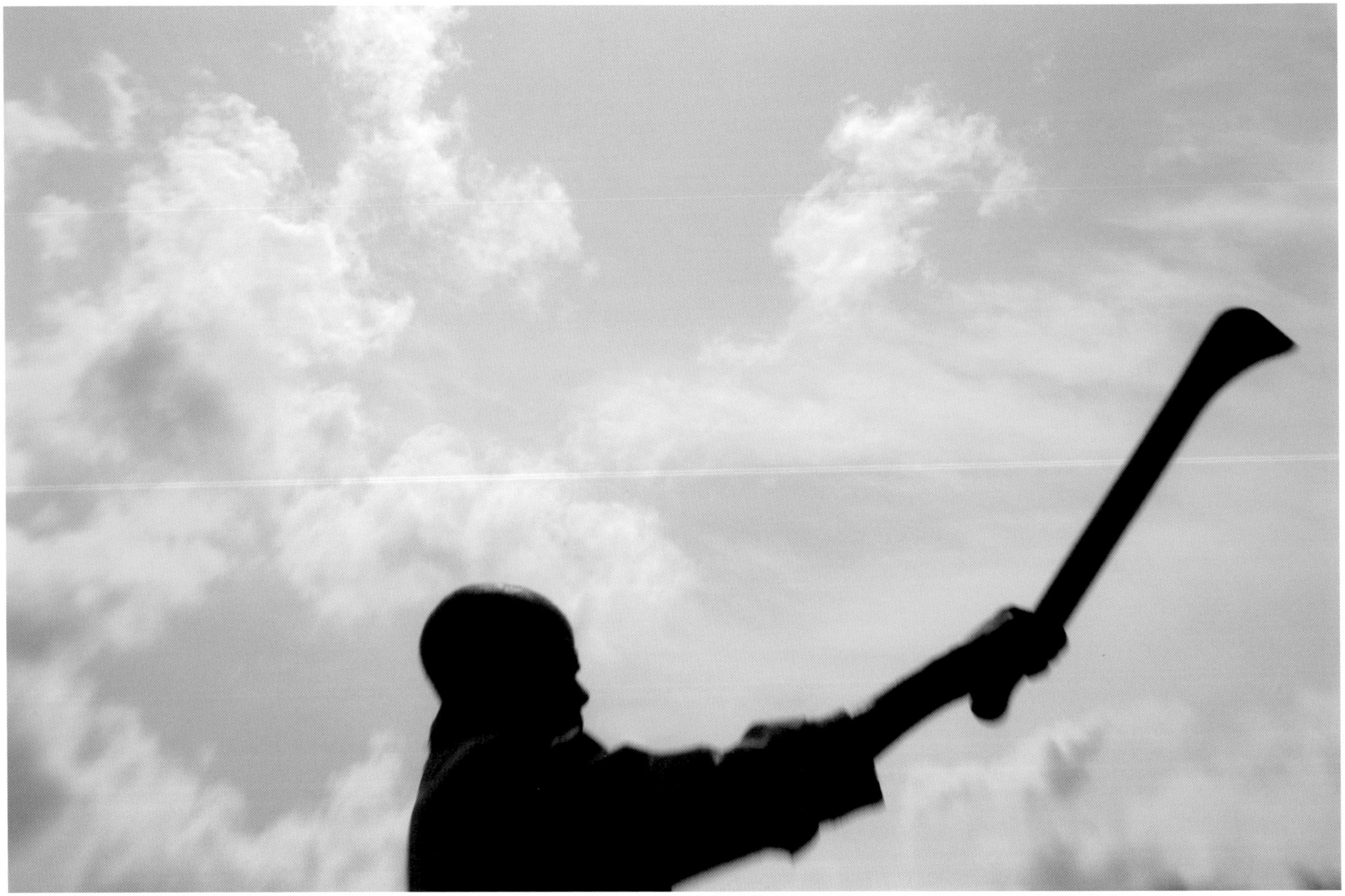

JACOB, AGE 12

One night I dreamed that robbers were coming to attack me, but I ran.
Both of them had knives for killing me. I was running back home
and found a big, big, dam and when the robbers were getting near that dam
there was the tall-grassed bush. So I hid away from those two robbers,
and they could not find any way to attack me.

GEOFFREY, AGE 10

I dreamed that I was going to dig in the garden to plant my mother’s crops.

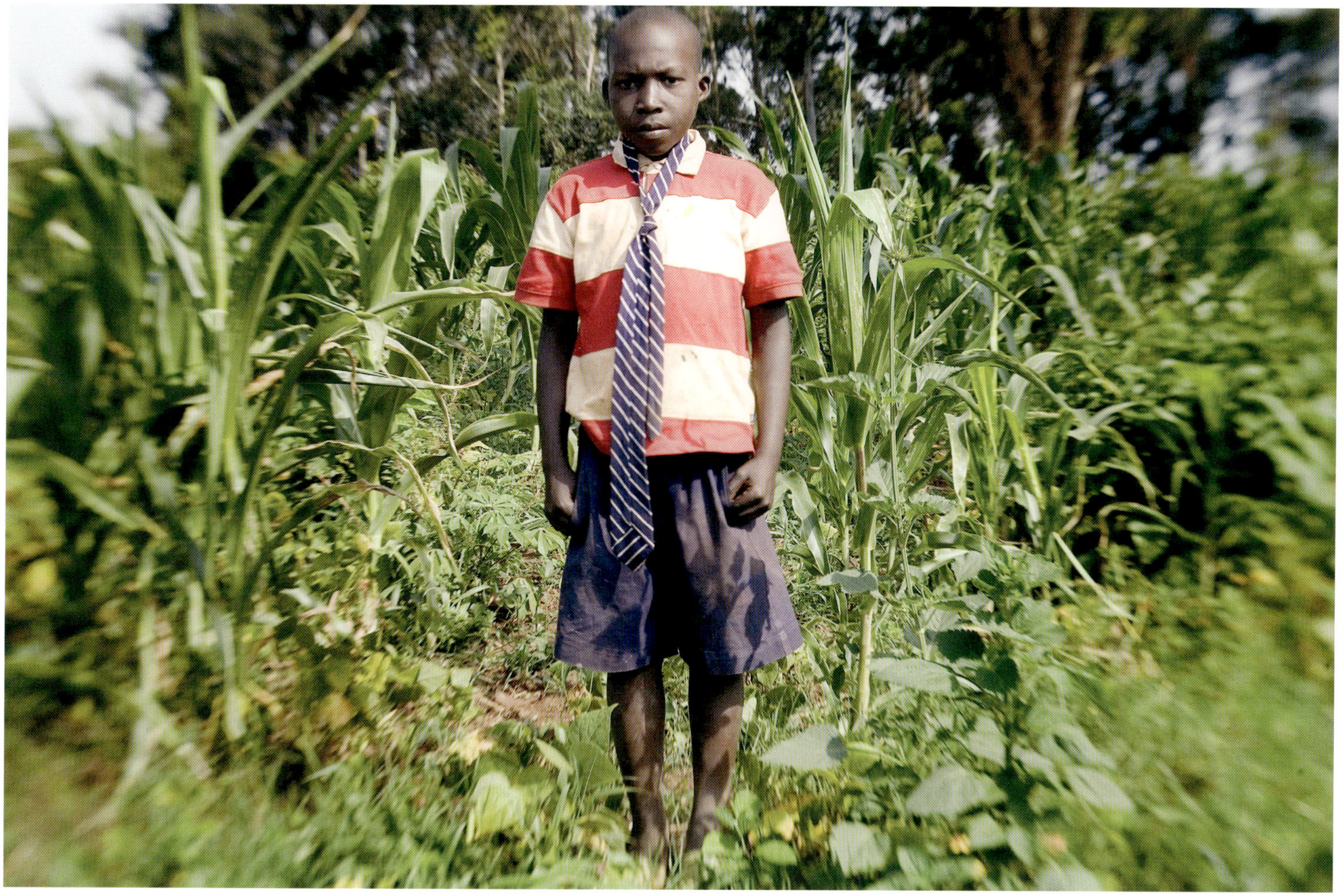

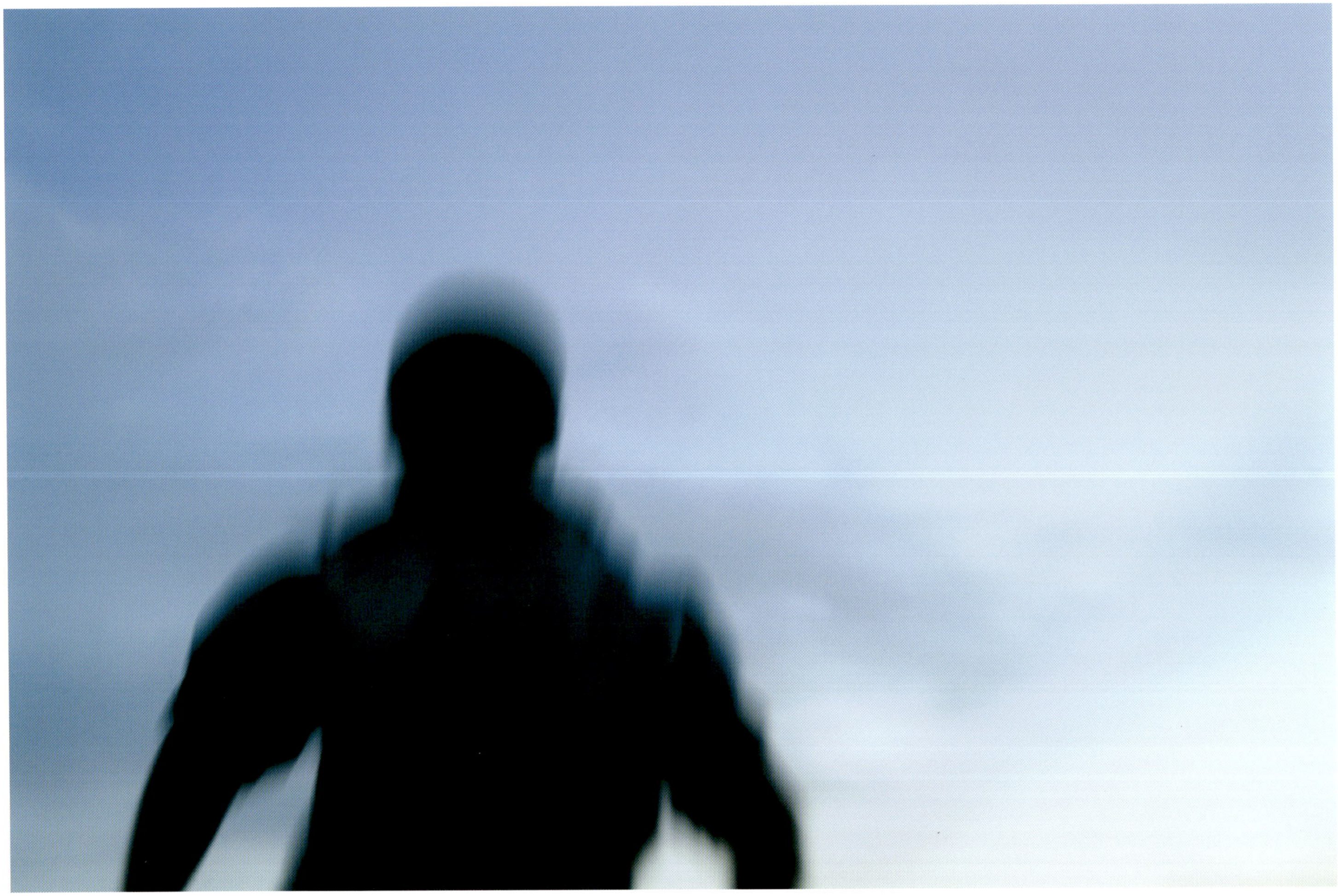

JAMES, AGE 12

I dreamed about when they were going to take us to war.
I was the leader of my team. There was a man who was president.
He was the one who commanded us to go and fight.

There were seven of us. That man gave us an airplane for war.

The enemy soldiers got a helicopter to come. It was going to kill all my soldiers.
We jumped out of our airplane. The blades of the helicopter started to come near us
but then my team won the war.

We went back to the base, and we made a party for my team.

TINA, AGE 7

When I sleep I see a cup and clothes.
I drink from the cup and I am wearing the clothes.

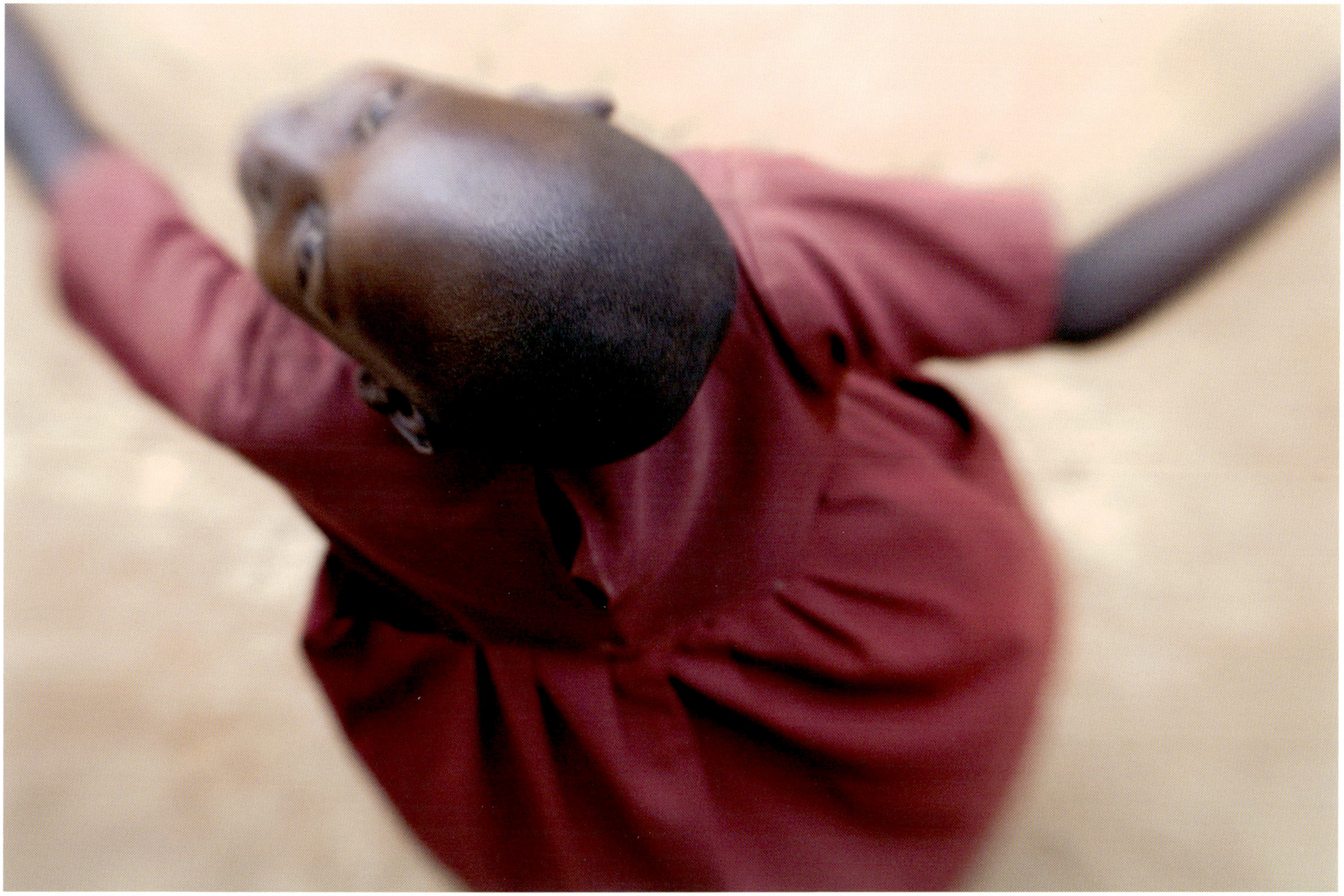

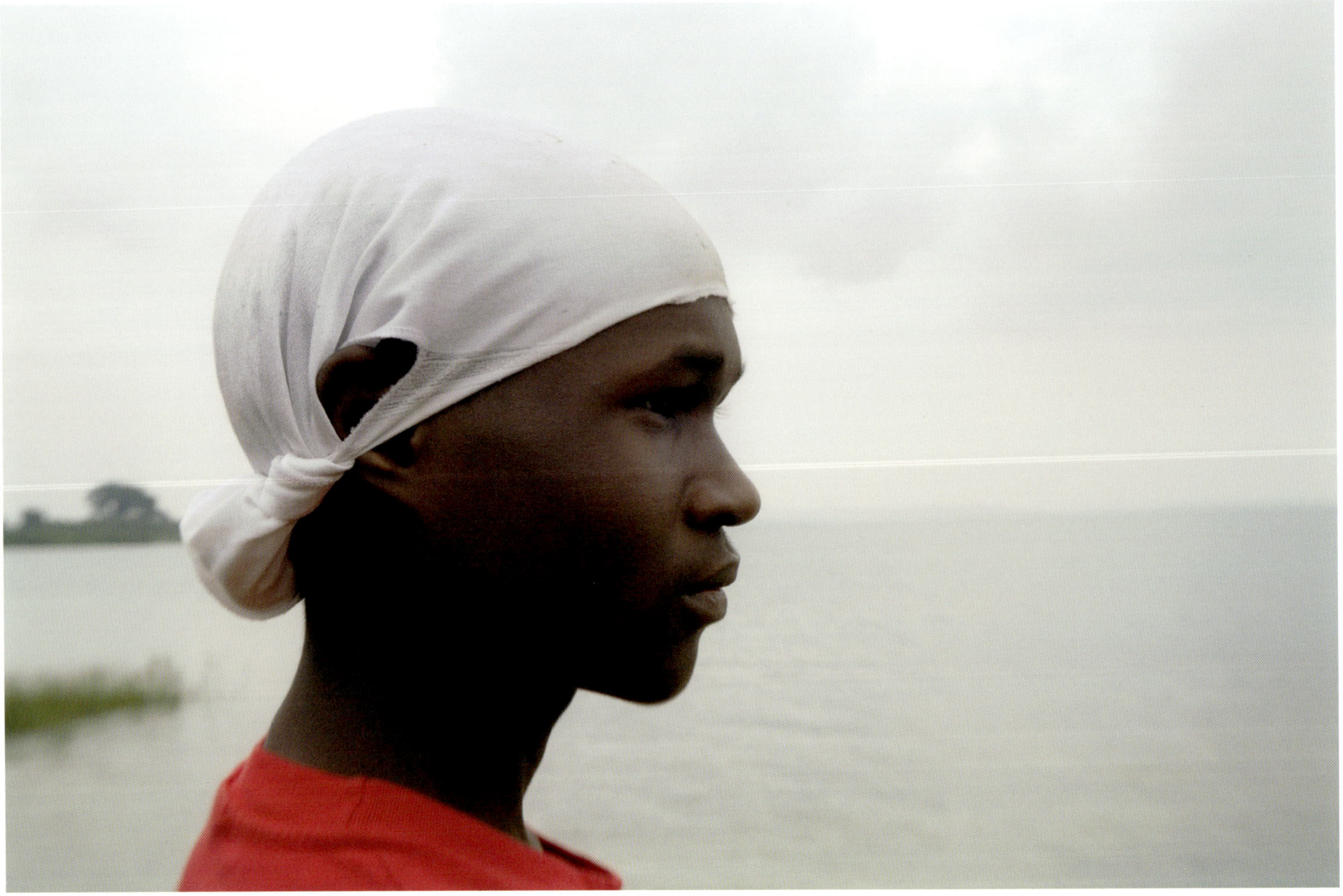

BILLY, AGE 16

I mostly dream that my father is one of the richest men in Kampala.

ROSETTE, AGE 16

I had a dream that I was in the airplane.
Then mummy told me to sit properly because I will fall down
out of the airplane, and I told her that I can't fall out of the airplane
because it is locked. Then I laughed and woke up.

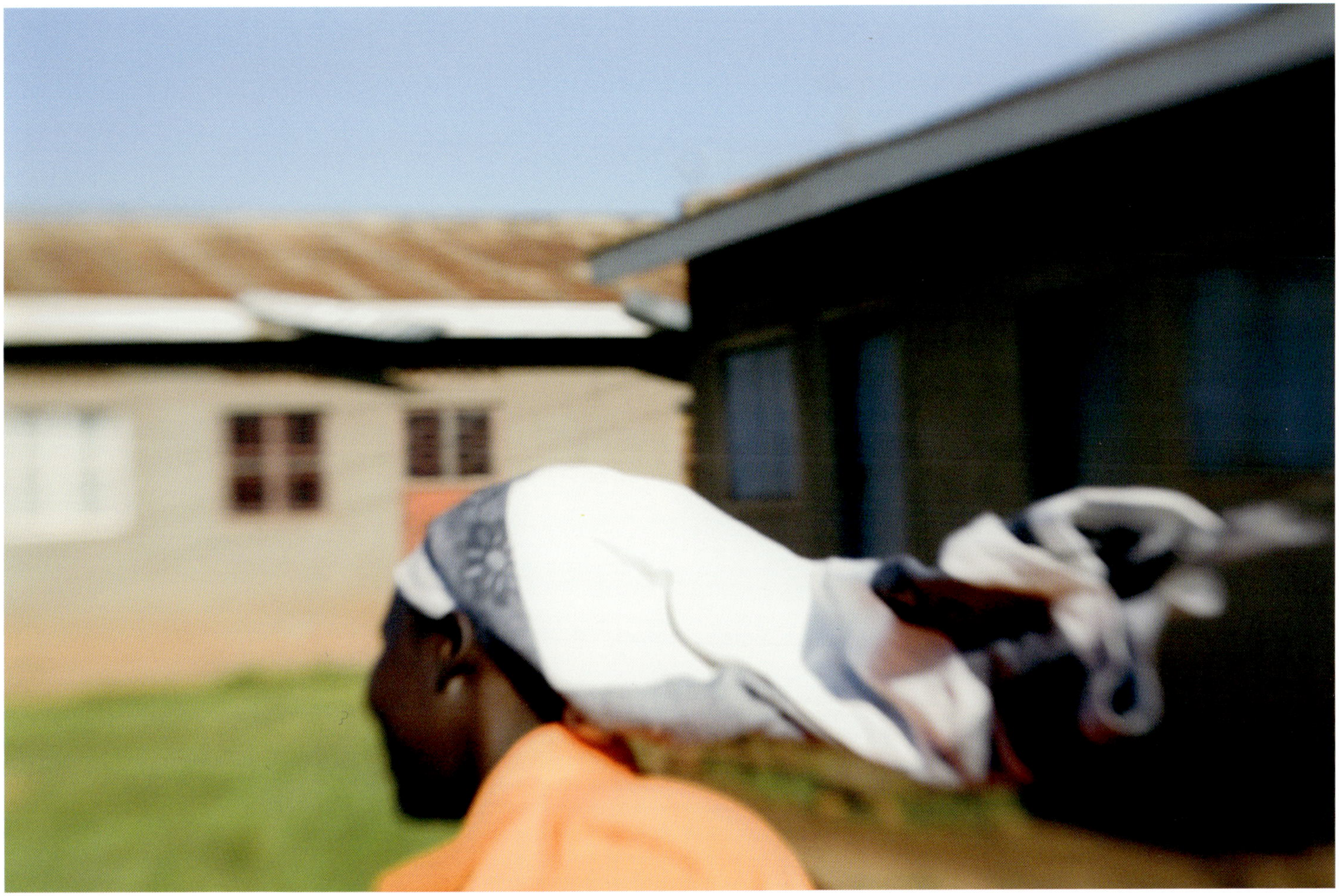

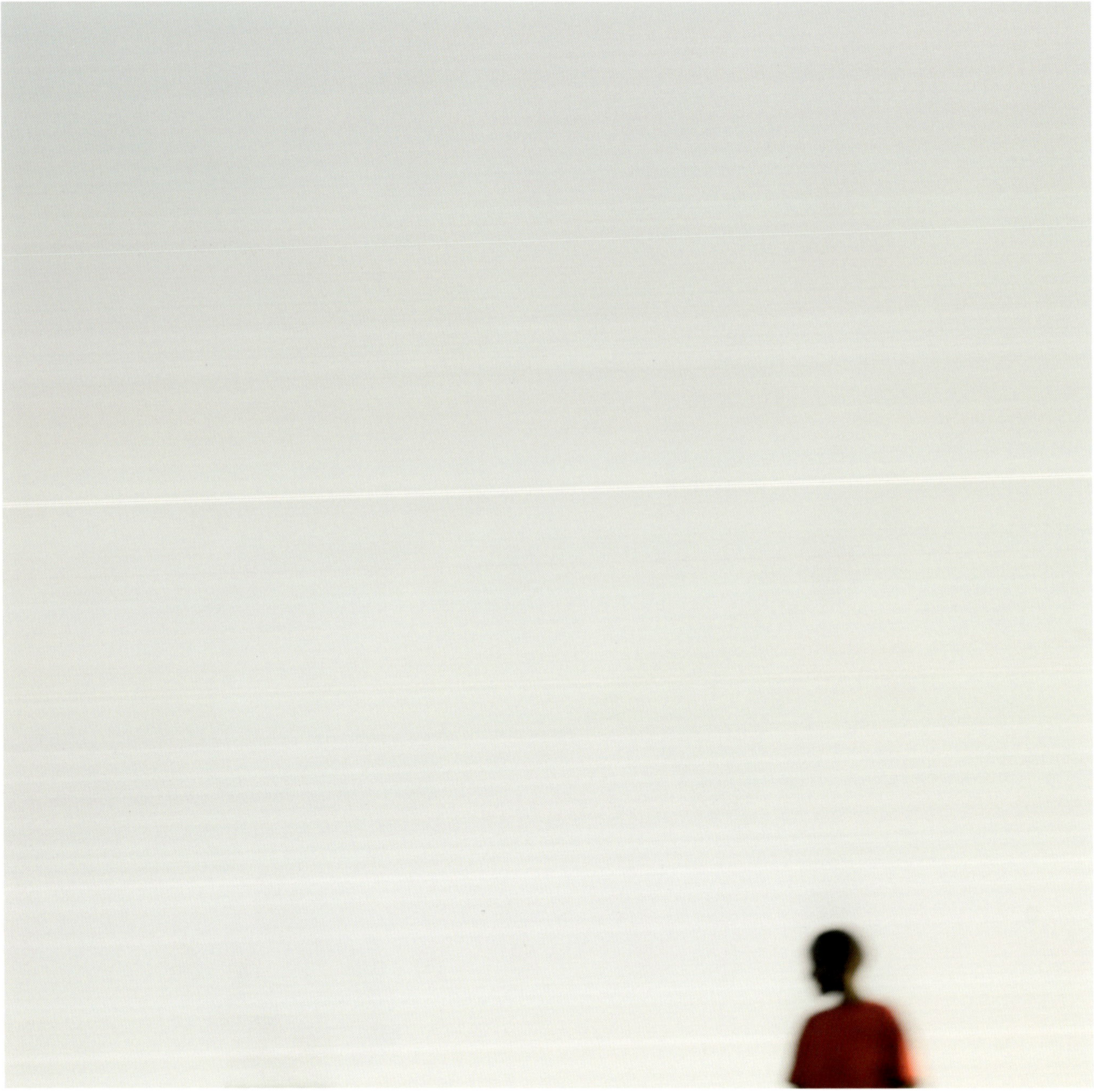

NAHIA, AGE 12

I dreamed that I fell in the lake.
Then I shouted at the water.

ALI, AGE 13

I dream I am driving a car.

I dream I am swimming.

I dream that a snake is biting me.

I dream a car has knocked me down.

I dream when I am on the bus and a lion is going to eat me.

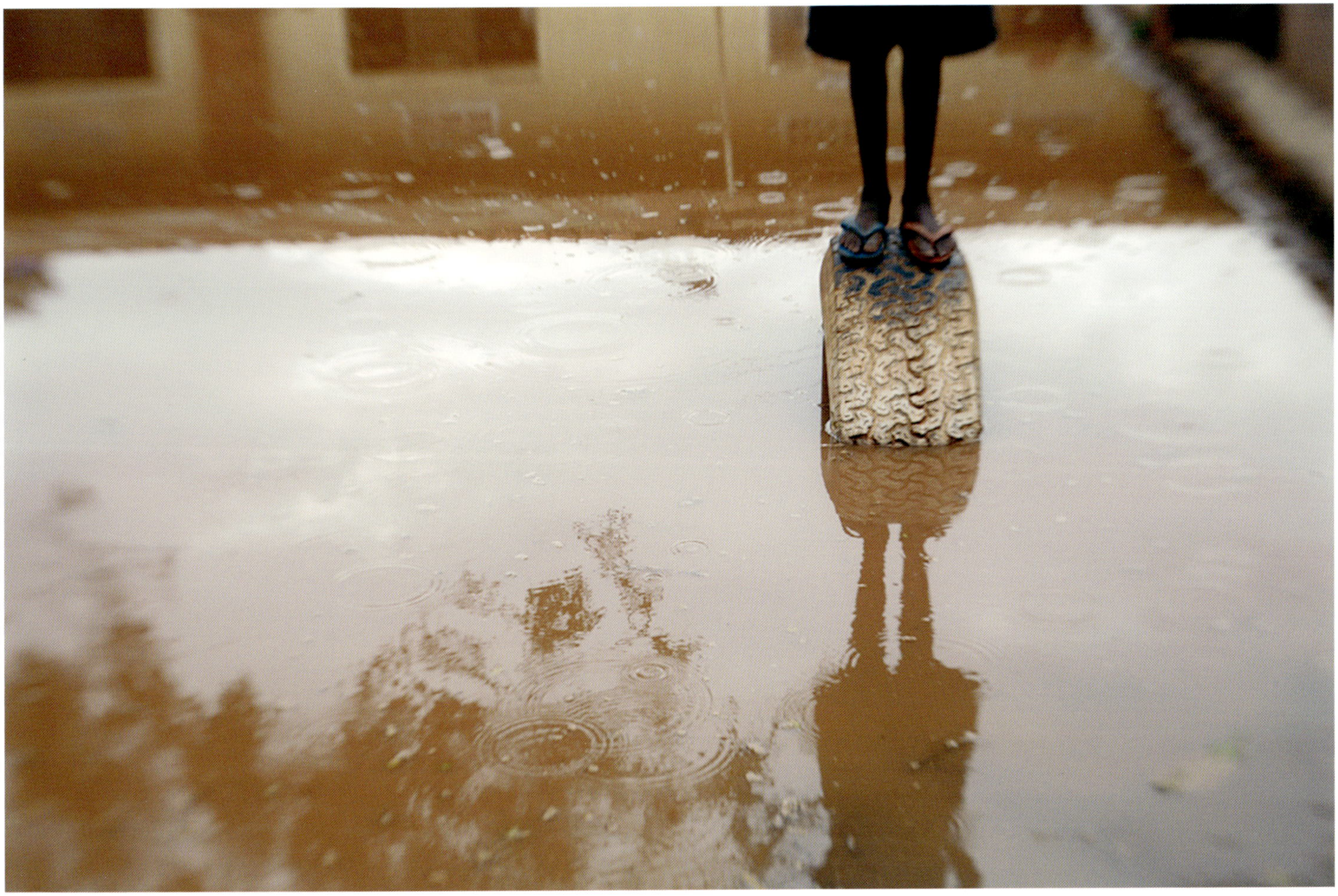

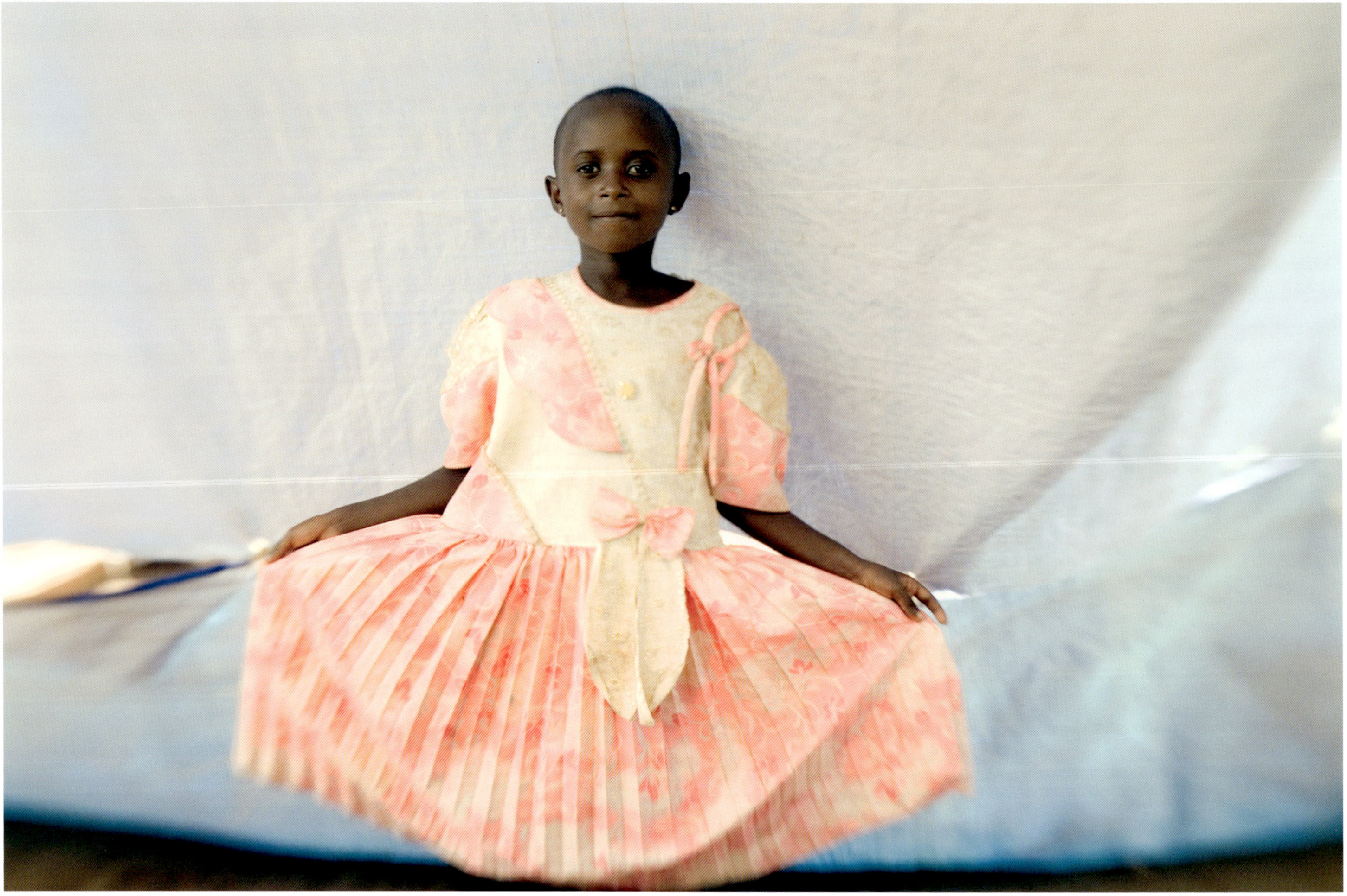

RHITA, AGE 7

I dreamed that my mother flew to America.

DOUGLAS, AGE 9

I was playing with my friend, and he pushed me into the lake. I started to swim, and my clothes got wet. After that I went back home, and my mom asked me where I had been.

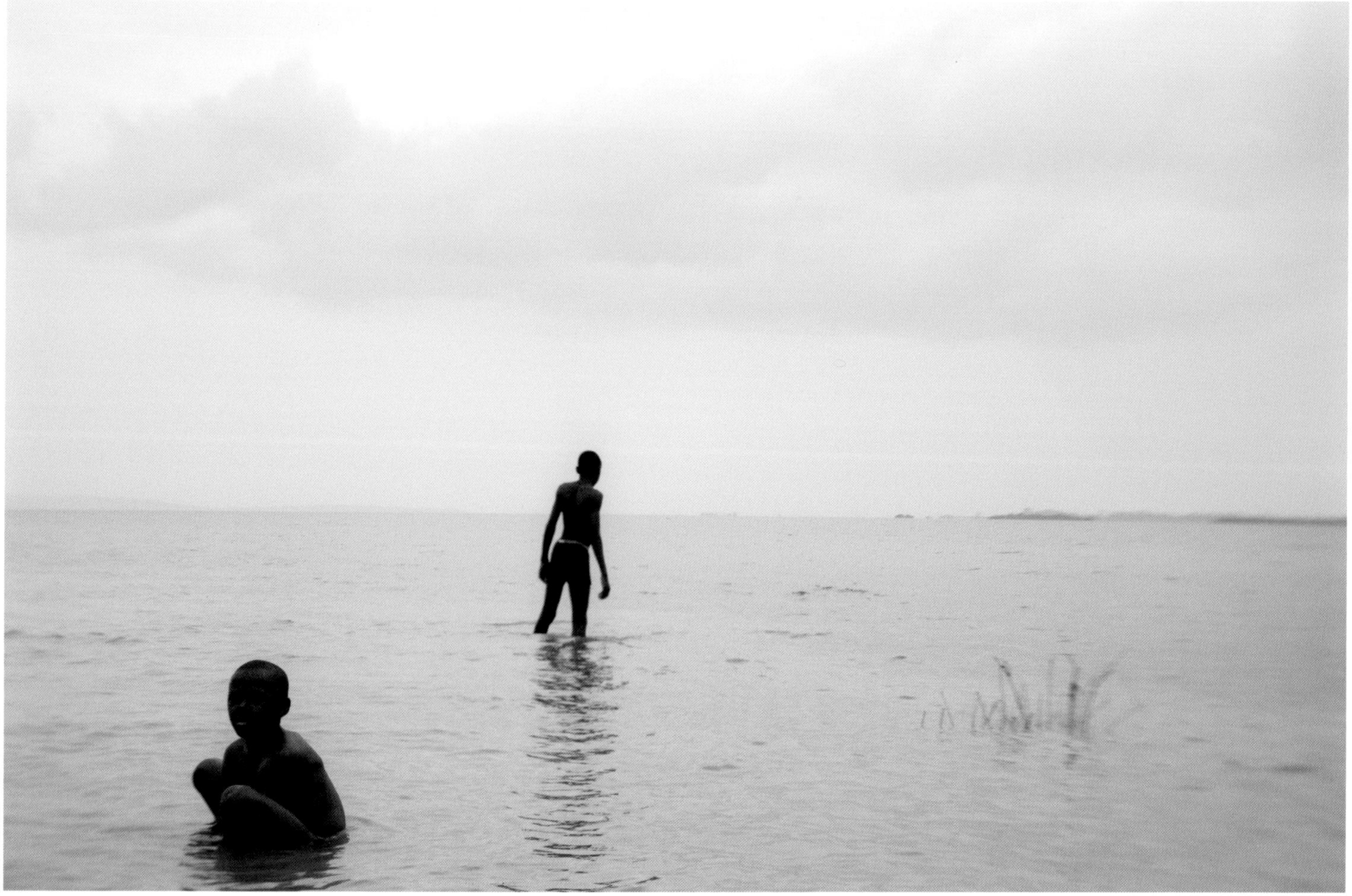

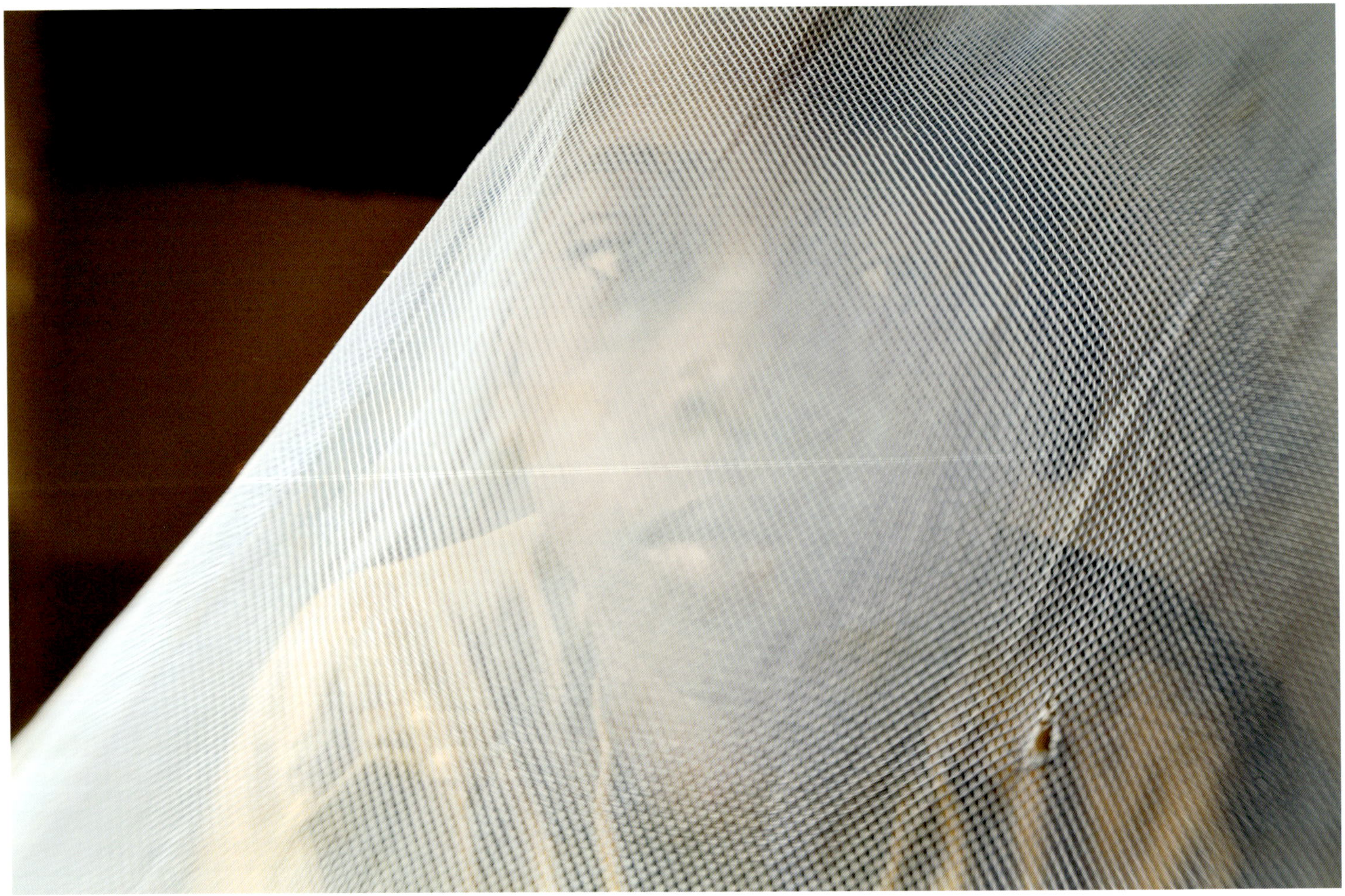

VINCENT, AGE 10

At night when I was sleeping, I had a horrible dream.
I saw a night dancer. He chased me all night. I was in the village,
and the only solution which I had was to run up to the house.
My big brothers came for my rescue, and they chased him away.
He went back to his home. He left behind bones of the dead.

NICHOLAS, AGE 12

I dreamt one night that I was flying in the air like a bird.
In that dream I was one of the Easter bunnies. I dreamt that my work was to treat sick children, not to supply eggs to the children. I could run, hop and fly, and I flew in the air to America and would go to every continent searching for sick children and of course, I was the fairy doctor and sometimes I flew in the daytime. But I could not finish my dream when I was waked up by my dormitory leader to go to school.

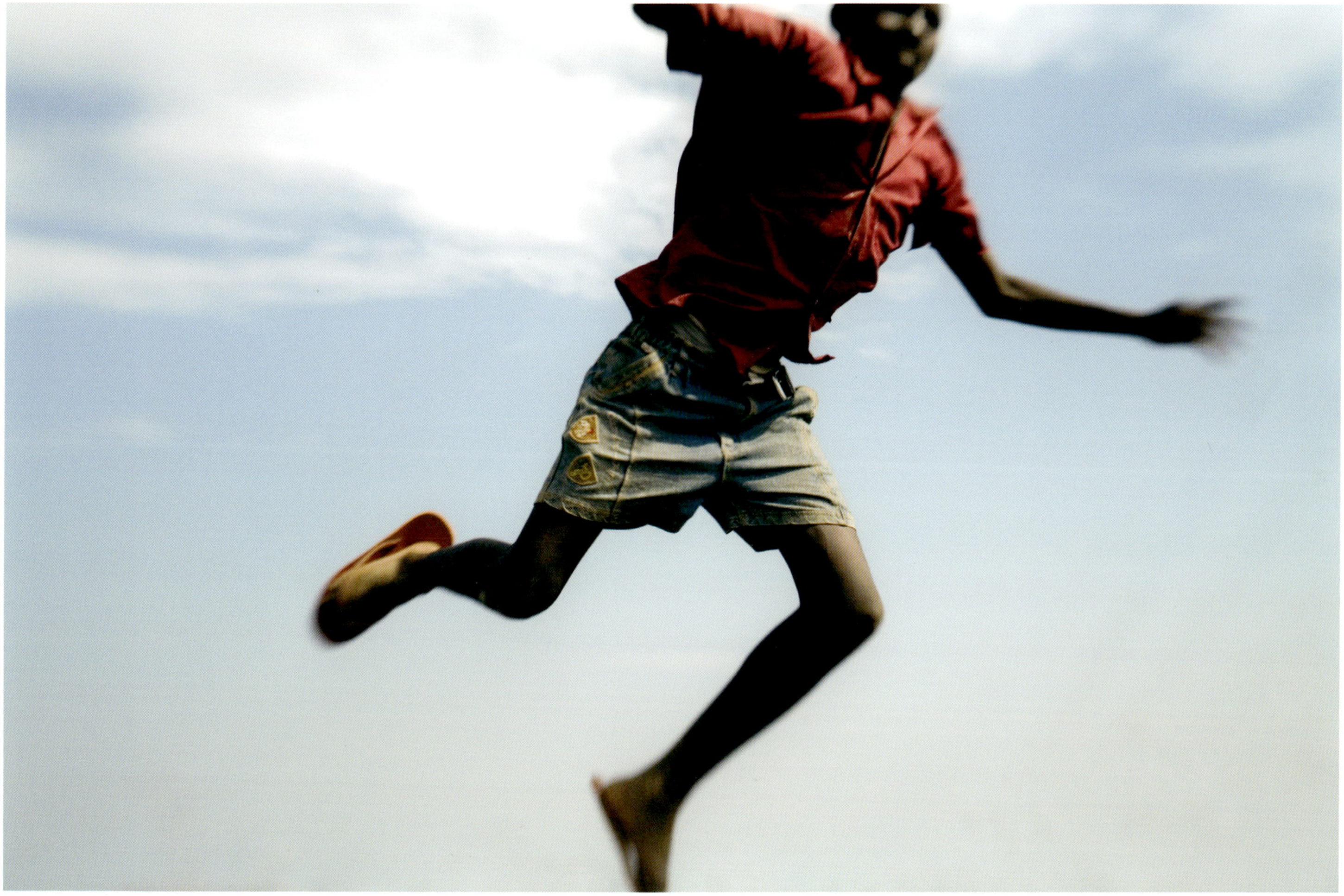

TUUKA MU

(reach in)

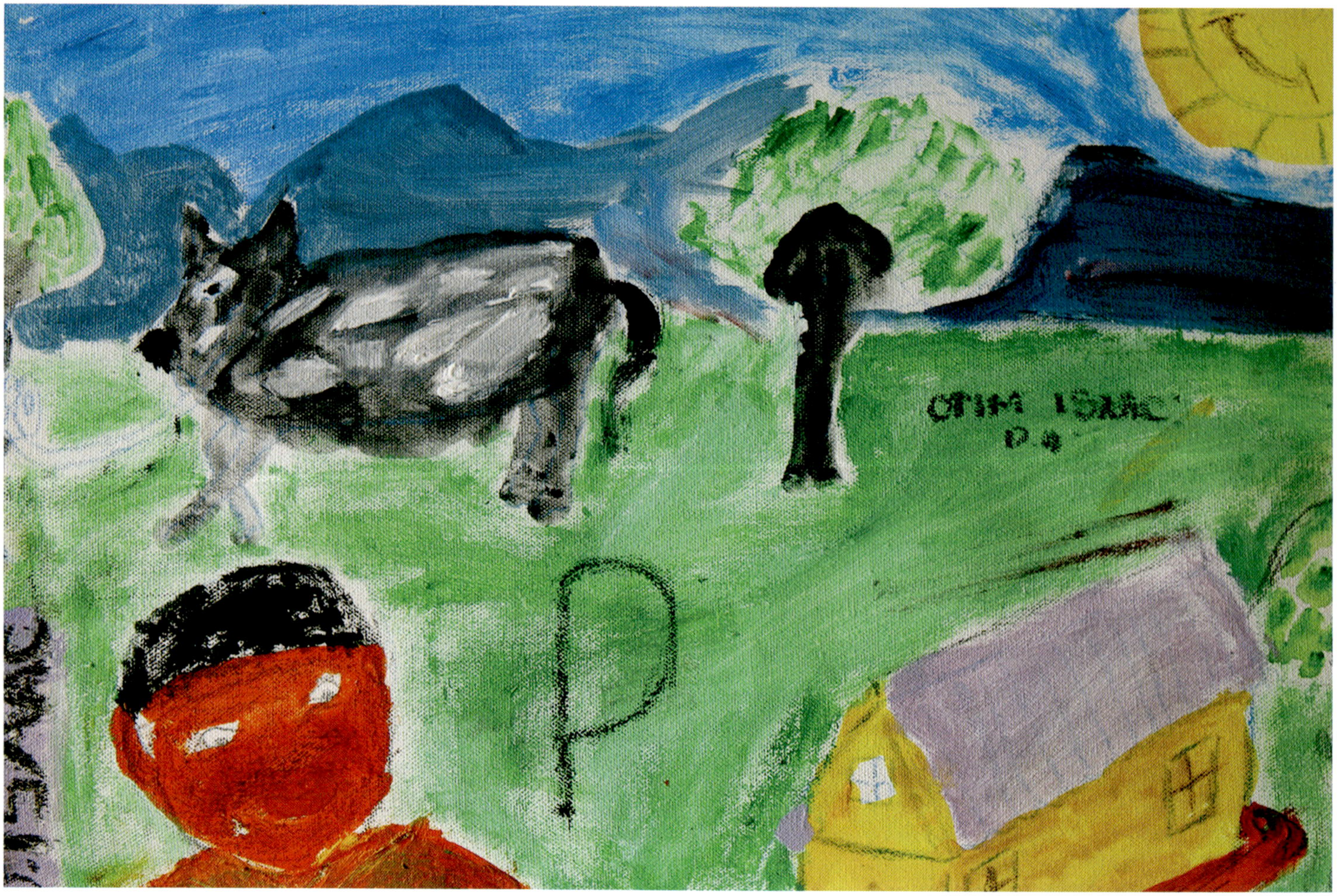
OTIM ISAAC

M. ANN THOMAS

A ten year old boy sits on a wooden bench in a simple room with chipped paint on the walls and red dirt on the concrete floor. He stares through the glassless window into a courtyard where dozens of children walk and talk, some holding hands, some smiling, some somber. He stares until a voice brings him back to the room. It is an American voice that says, "use the paints any way you want but make a picture—a picture of things you know—of things you remember." The quiet child looks down at beautiful new paints, clean brushes and a pile of canvas on which to paint. He sees other children beginning to work. Some talk, but most are quiet as their memories come to life with beautiful strokes of oranges, greens and blues. Isaac begins, knowing already what he will paint: it is a picture he has carried for several years inside his head. He works carefully, and others notice his intensity. He rehearses the lines before committing them to the canvas; it is important that it be done right. The adults look on, wondering what will emerge from this young man.

Isaac draws a bus: not just any bus, but the bus he wishes he could have ridden. His mother and father had been on the bus. Isaac's aunt was on it, too. She is the one who later told him of the gunshots, and the death of his parents. He has seen this bus only in his imagination, but he knows it well.

In the days that follow, Isaac makes several pictures on canvas, on paper, on fabric and in the sand. His pictures change from graphically violent images to more beautiful, colorful scenes of growth and people. Through drawing and then through words, he begins to release his traumatic memories and discover ways to communicate his pain and sadness. His art enables him to regain control of a situation which had overwhelmed him and left him helpless. Set down on a simple piece of paper, the feelings are contained, framed and manageable.

Isaac is eventually able to illustrate the story and his wishes. Several of his final pieces of art show a beautiful house tucked away from people, with a long driveway that is lined with trees. Armed men and dogs guard the driveway to keep the family safe. They have a car, so no one has to ride the buses again. The family sits and eats together in safety.

The body is amazingly well-equipped to go to battle to protect itself when faced with danger, but the aftermath can be devastating as the mind struggles to make sense of the experience. Trauma keeps children from growing emotionally, socially, academically, and in some cases even physically. Experiences of such enormity stunt the developmental process as the mind shifts into survival mode: it becomes hypersensitive and fully alerted to future danger, while its ability to trust people wanes and the capacity to feel and express joy is virtually eliminated. Only when children can feel safe enough to integrate their experiences and release their intense feelings will they fully heal.

Many of the orphans at Saint Mary Kevin Orphanage Motherhood tell of feeling "wounded," (the word they most often use to describe their pain and loss) but also of feeling "encouraged" (the word they choose to describe how they feel loved and supported by the school community). The orphanage is a very safe place; it offers structure, predictability and a loving staff. But children outnumber adults, and as a result the children have limited opportunities to engage in healing activities. The amazingly talented team from America arrived with beautiful new crayons, paints and toys—tools the children so desperately needed to begin to repair their broken hearts. In a short time, many remarkable children found their voices and began to take control of their memories and, in the process, to turn their focus to dreams of the future.

When we dream, our brain rejuvenates itself and sorts through our experiences. We use the same word—to dream—to describe our strong conscious desires and goals. Psychological trauma takes a toll on both types of dreams. Traumatized children can be troubled by re-occurring nightmares at night while they struggle to feel hope or make plans during the day.

The images collected here represent children at different levels of healing as they explore both kinds of dreams. For some the dreams are about protection, escape and changing the past. For others the dreams are about strength, honor and opportunity, a sign that curiosity has returned and that the children are learning to cope with their trauma. These dreams, whatever their story, give us an insight into the experience of orphanhood. We see children who have traveled on a long journey. Children, who enter the orphanage wounded, feel encouraged to explore their trauma through art, and can then dream of a richer, fuller life.

Just as Gloria's camera captures the dignity of life even under distress, this collection of artwork transcends pain and psychological trauma and helps us see what it means to reach inside, to dream and to live.

M. Ann Thomas is a clinical social worker and Registered Play Therapist Supervisor at Operation Breakthrough in Kansas City, Missouri. She worked with the children in Uganda as a member of the Change the Truth team. Issac's guardian gave permission for the use of his story.

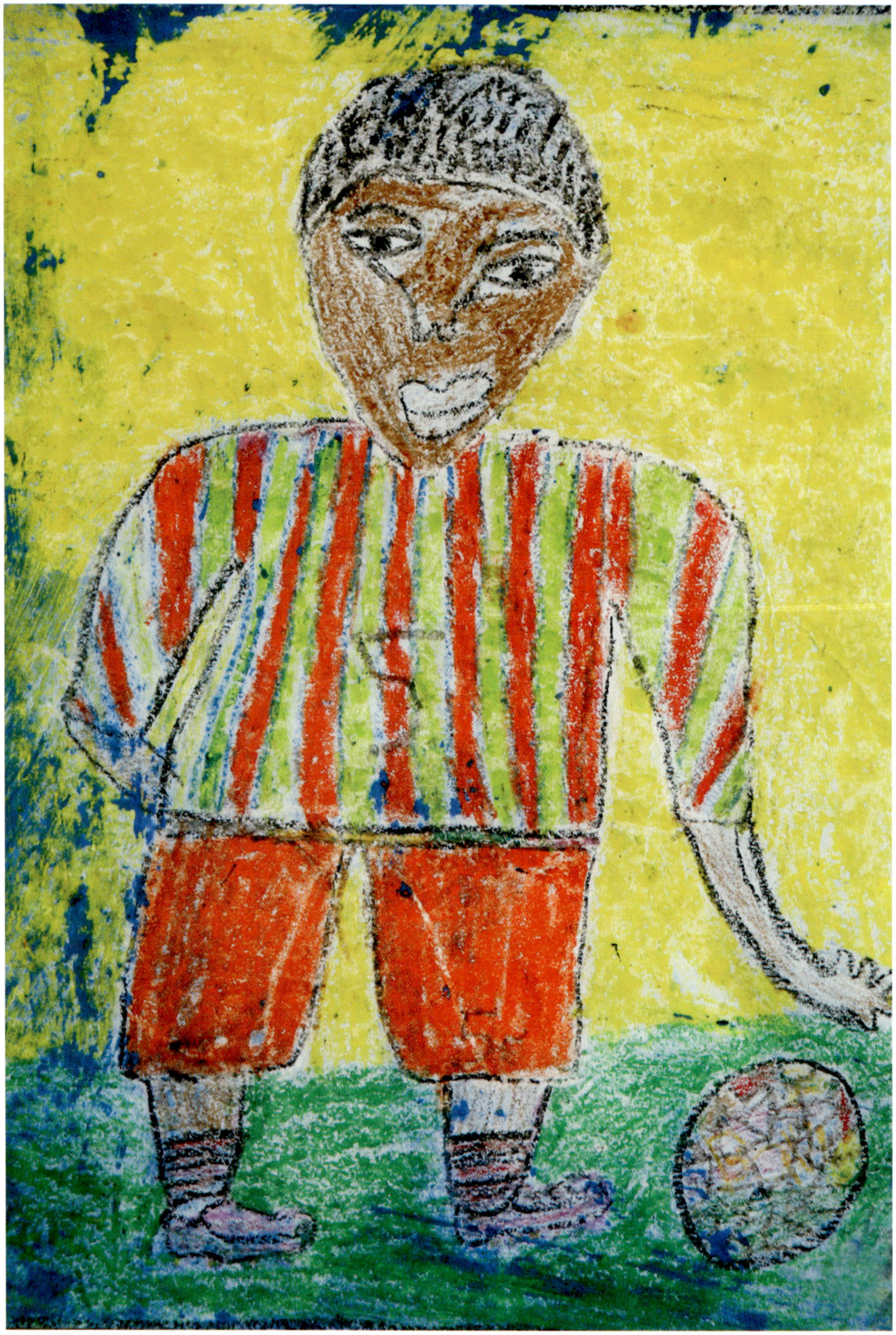

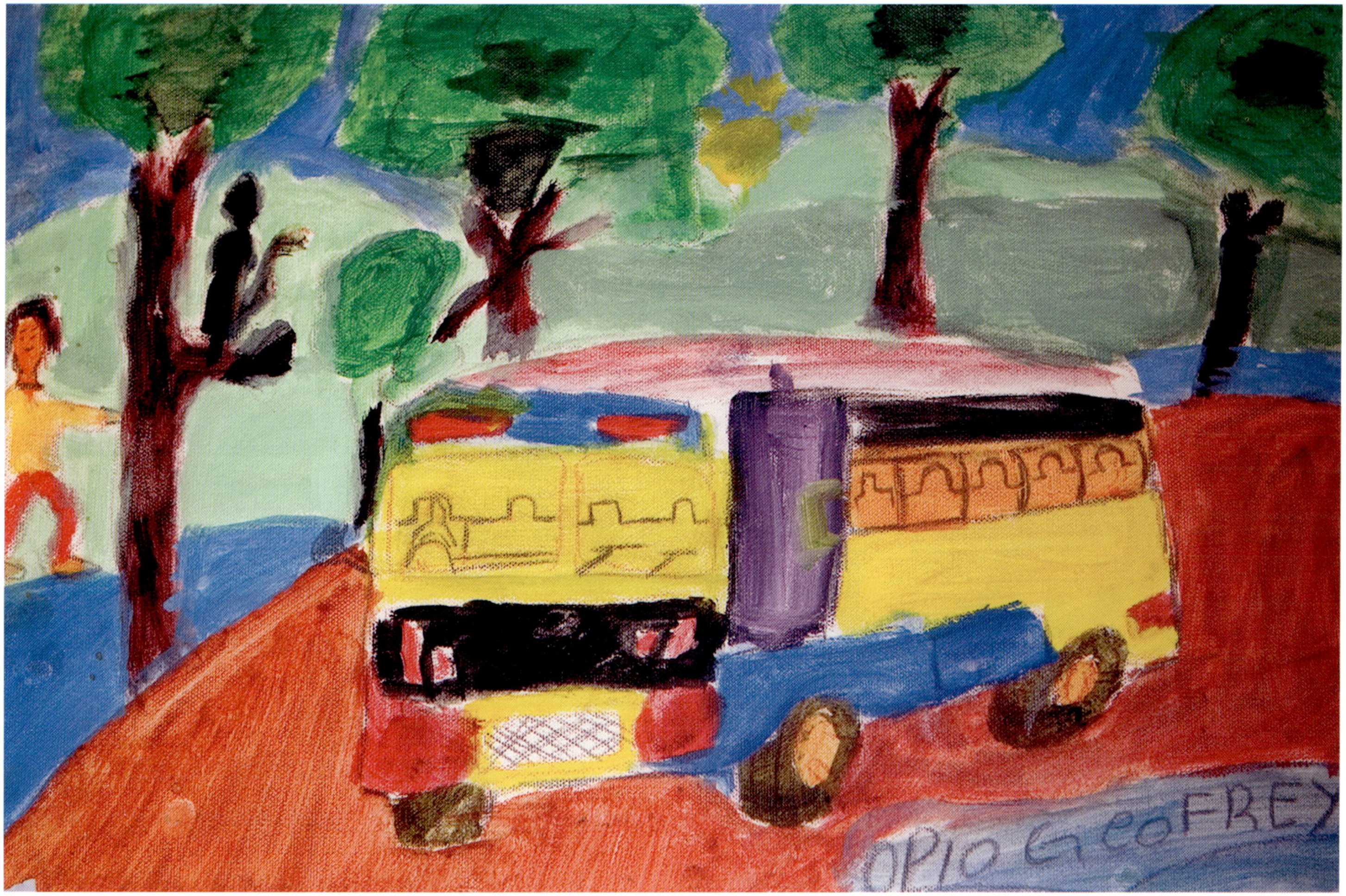
OPIO GEOFREY

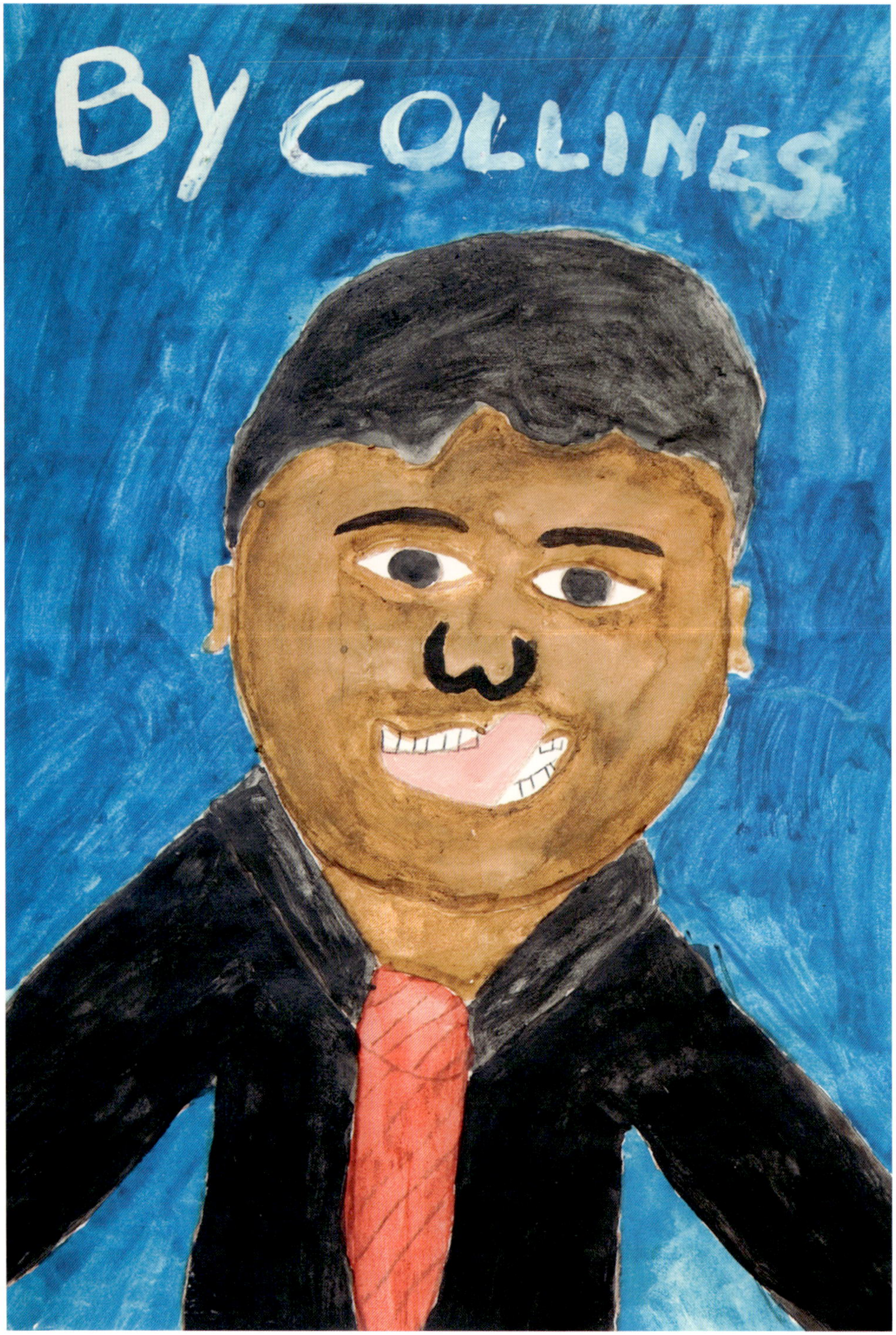
BY COLLINES

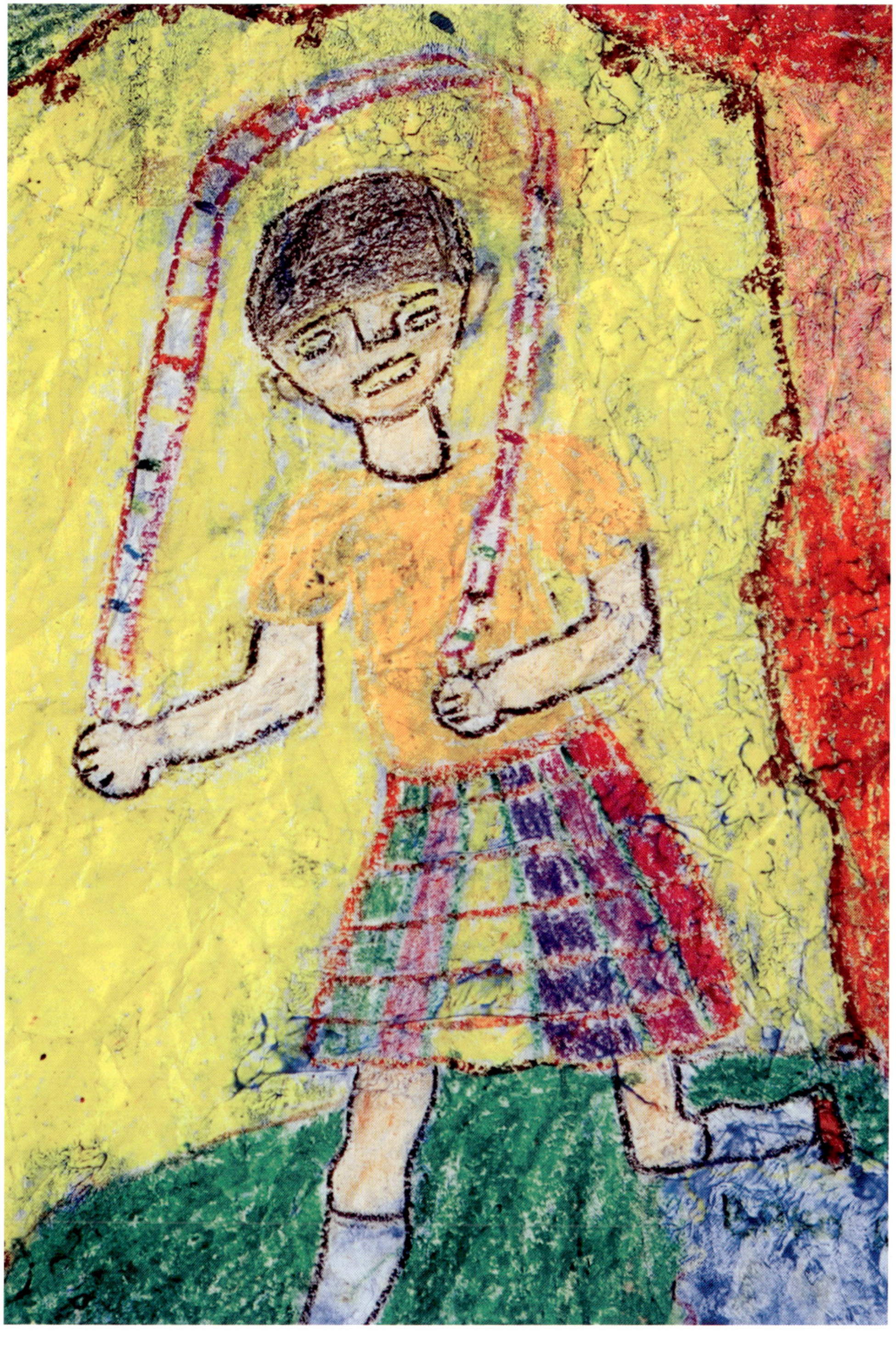

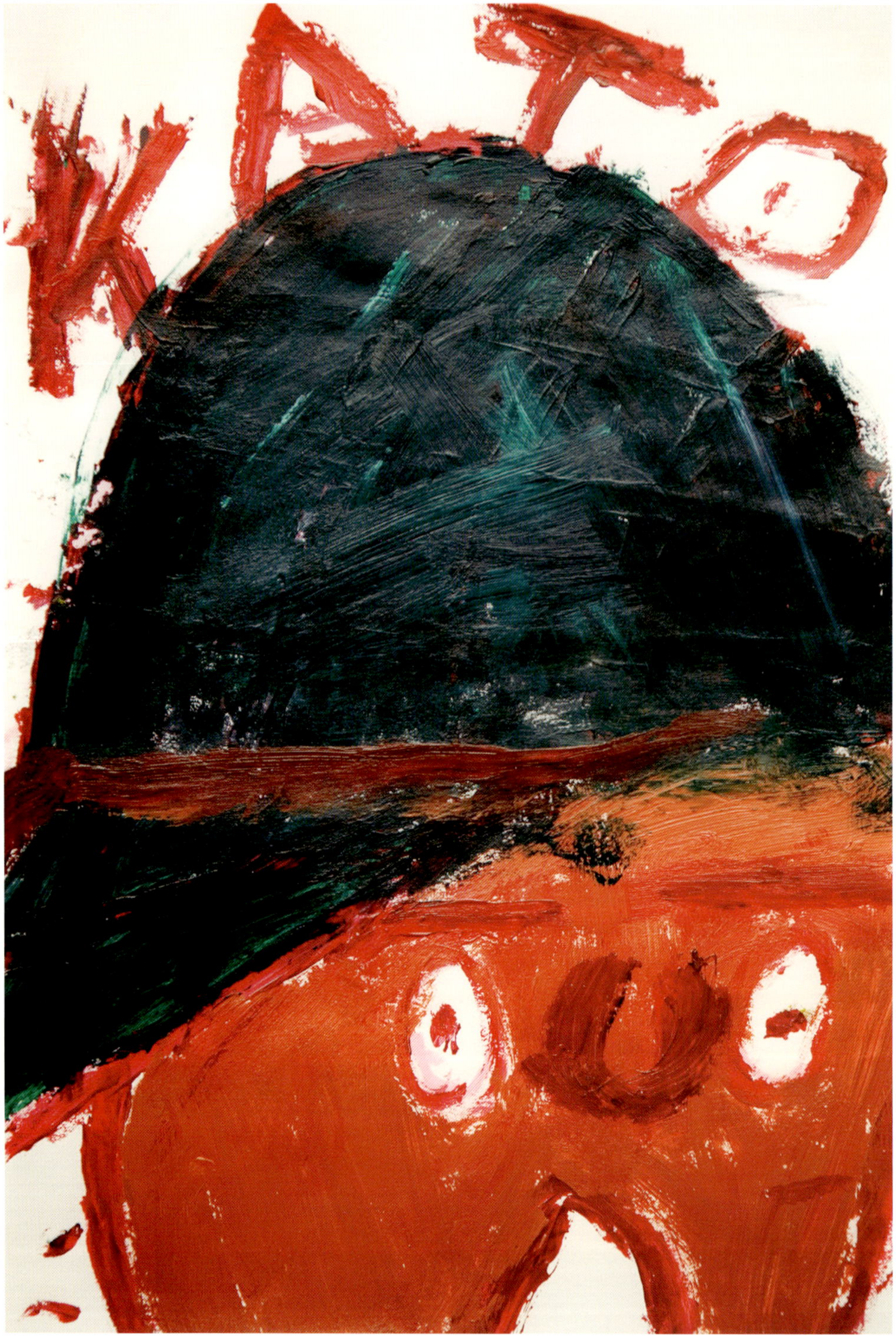
KATO

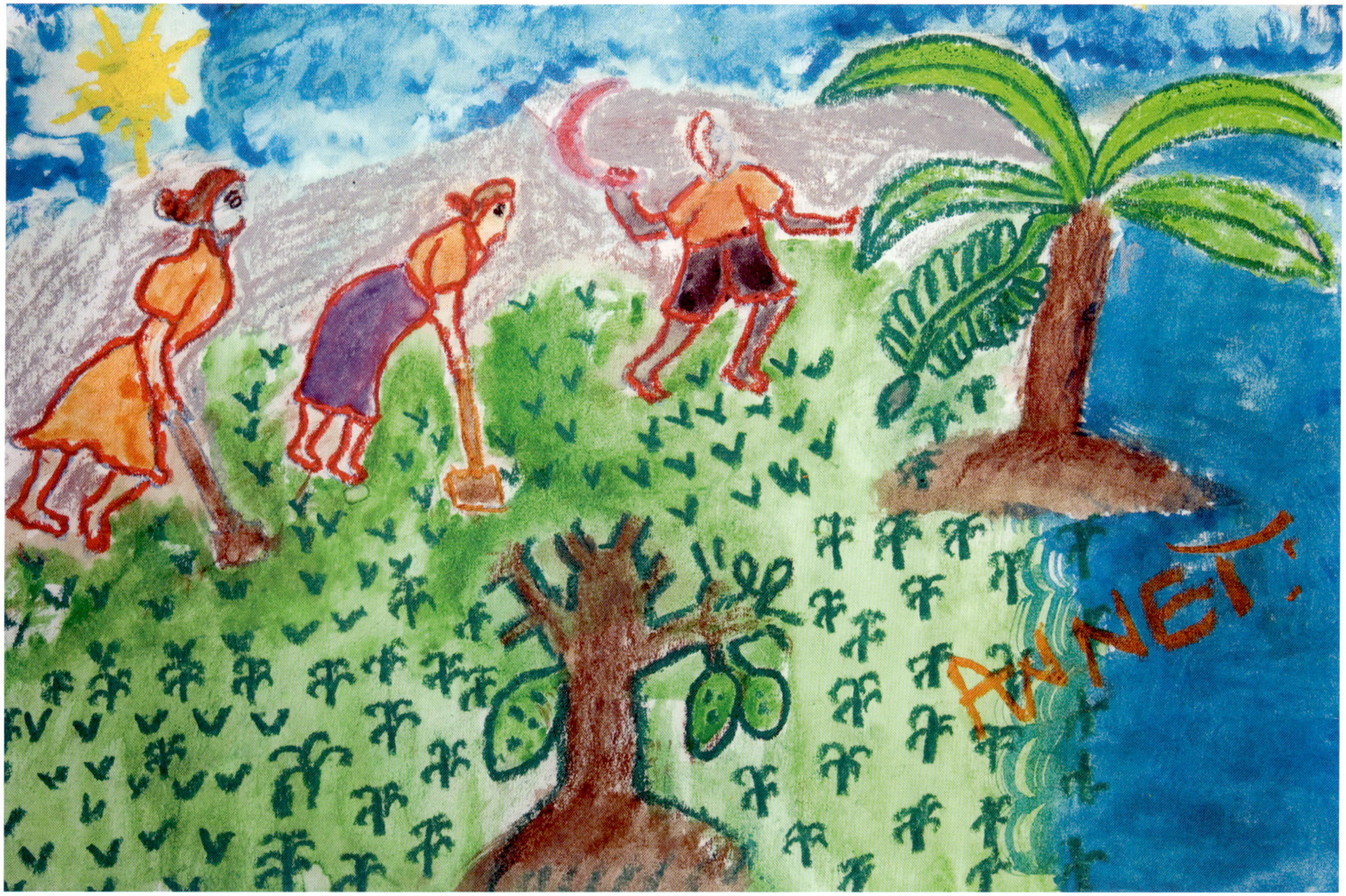
ANNET

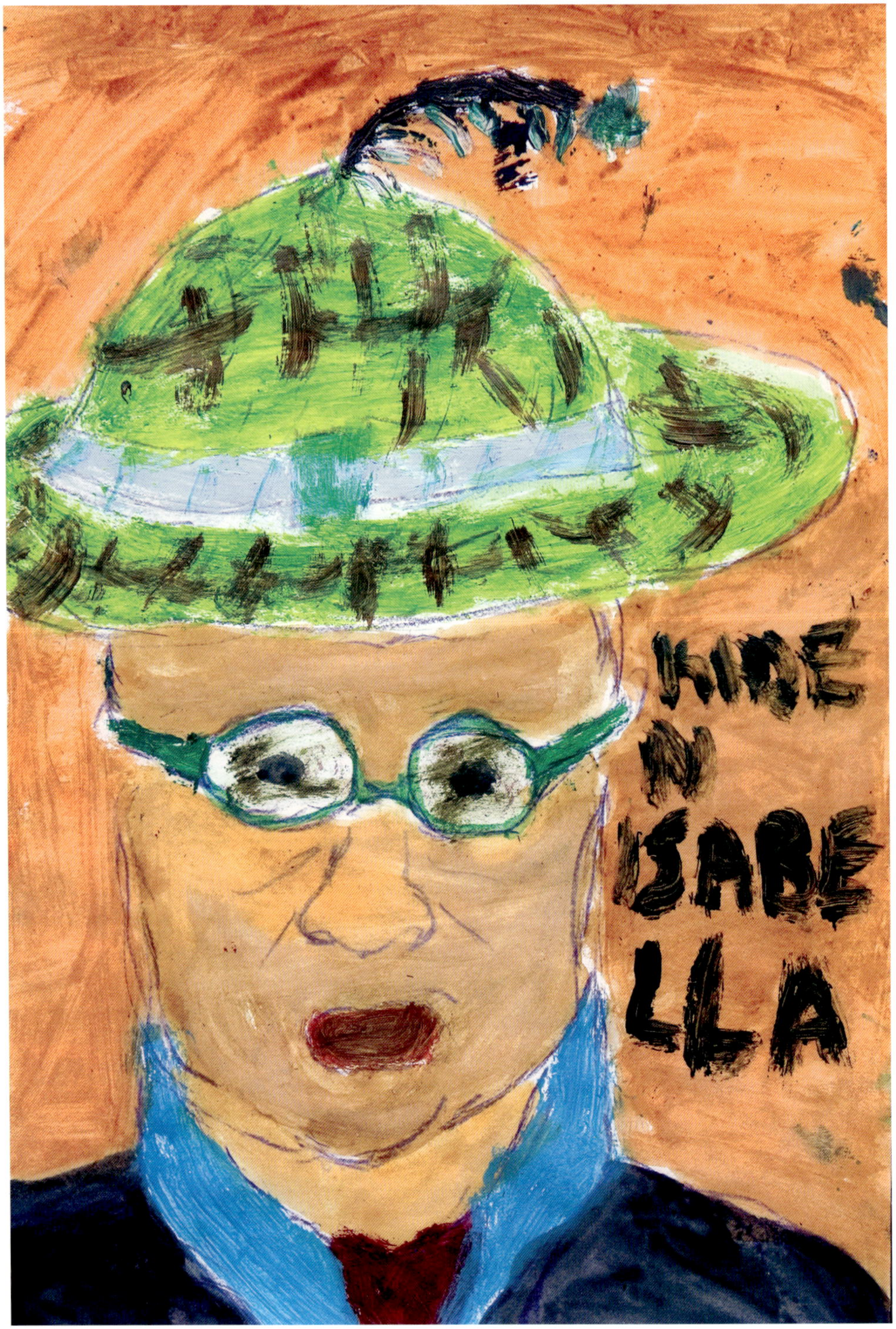
ISABE
LLA

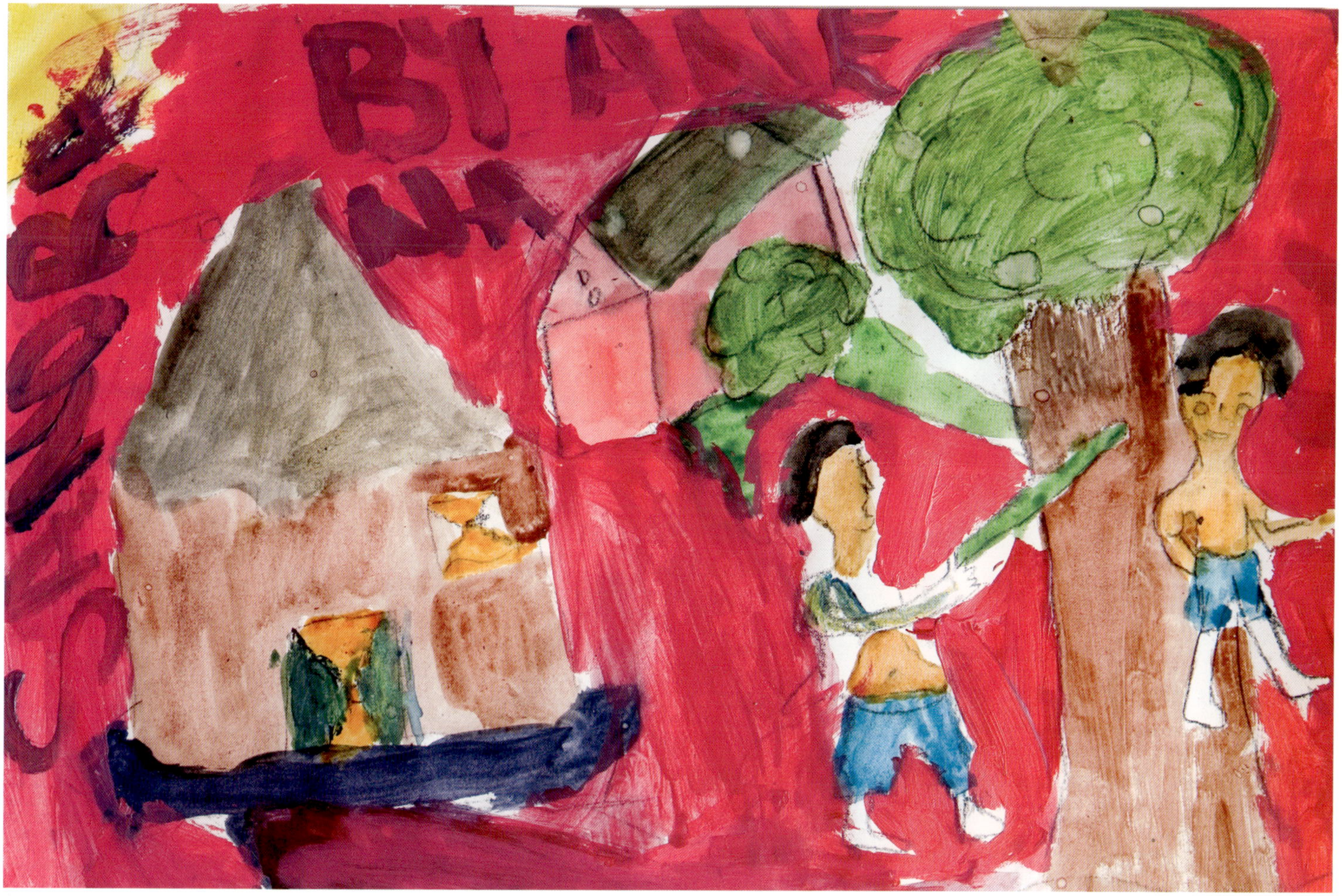

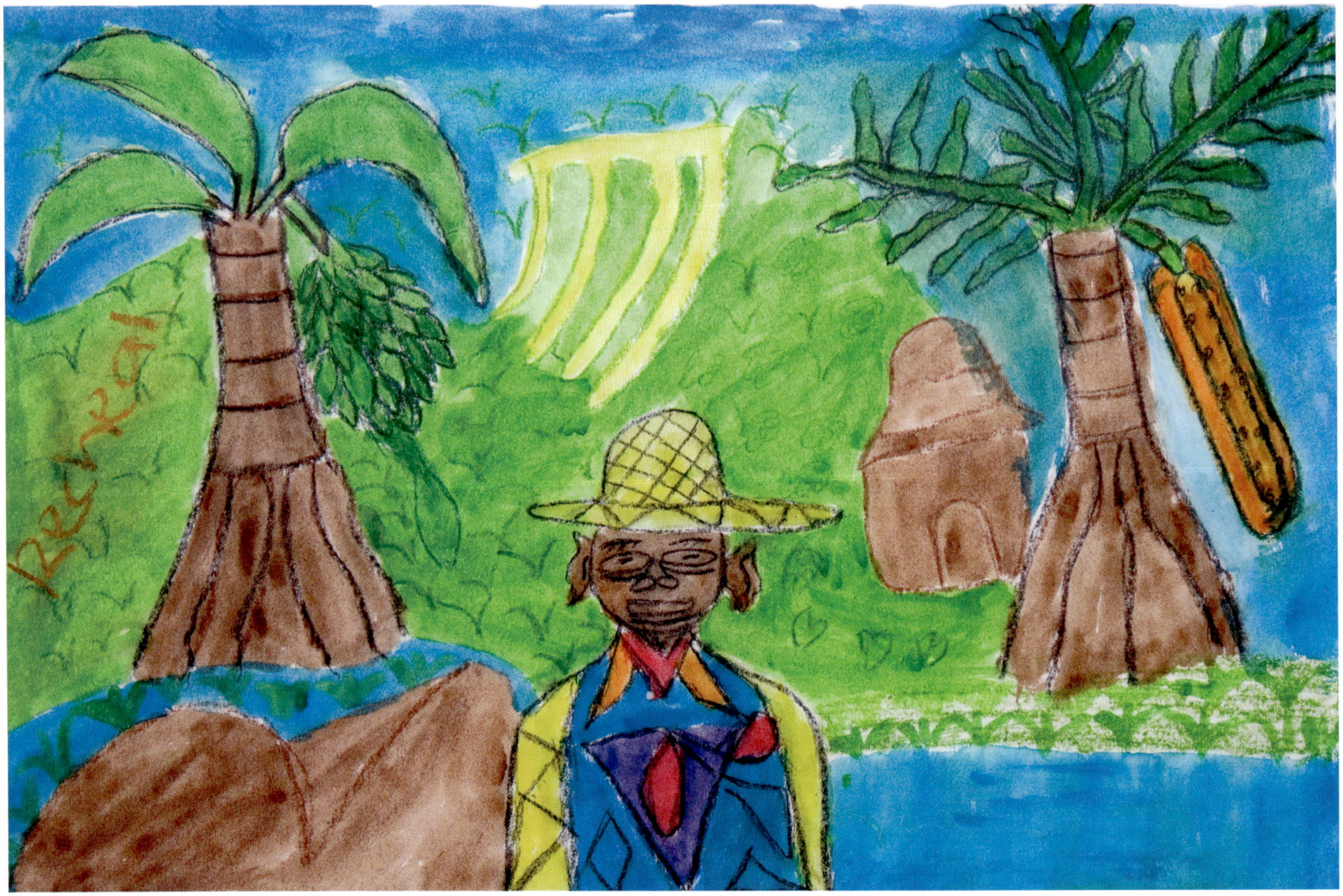

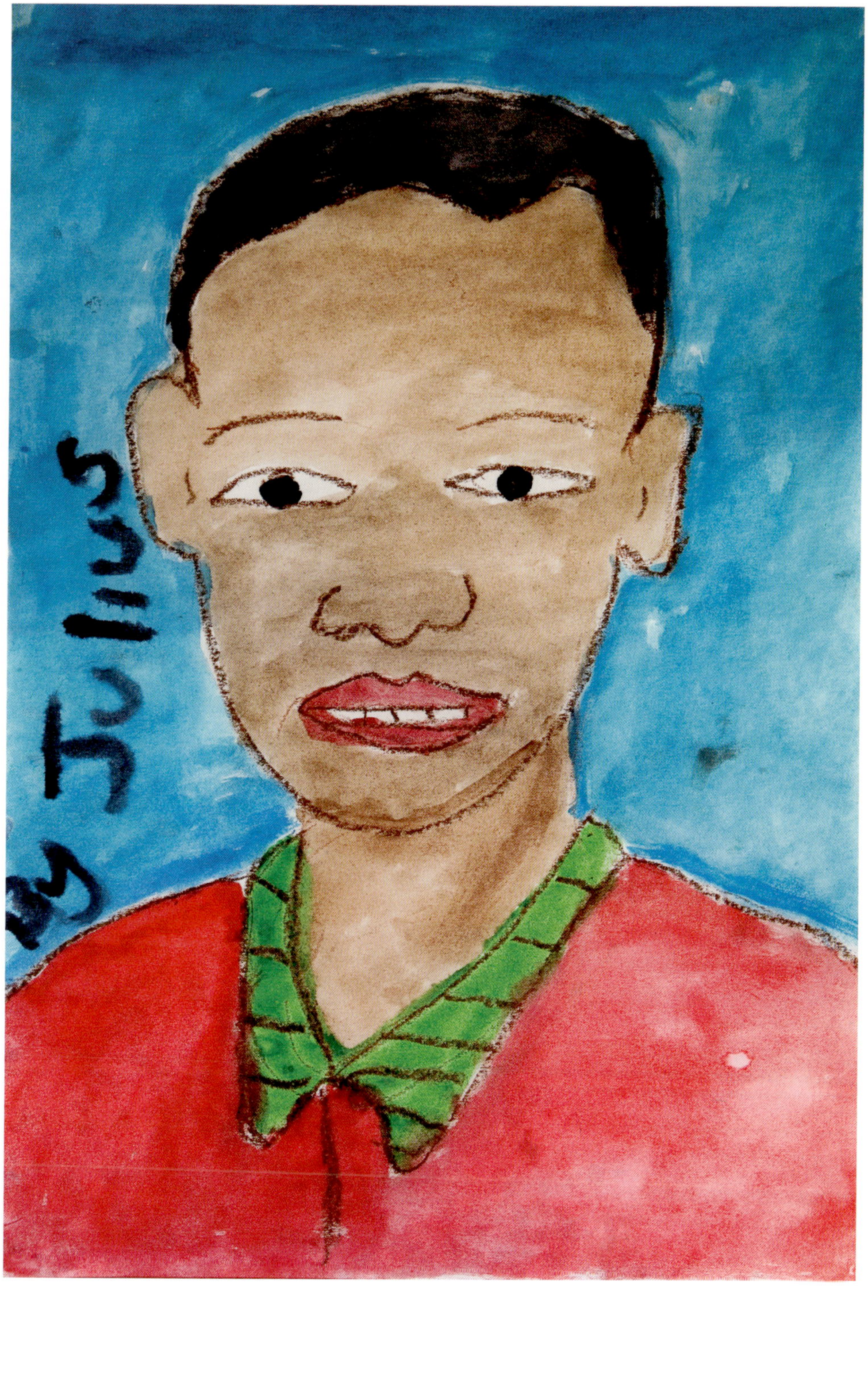
By Julius

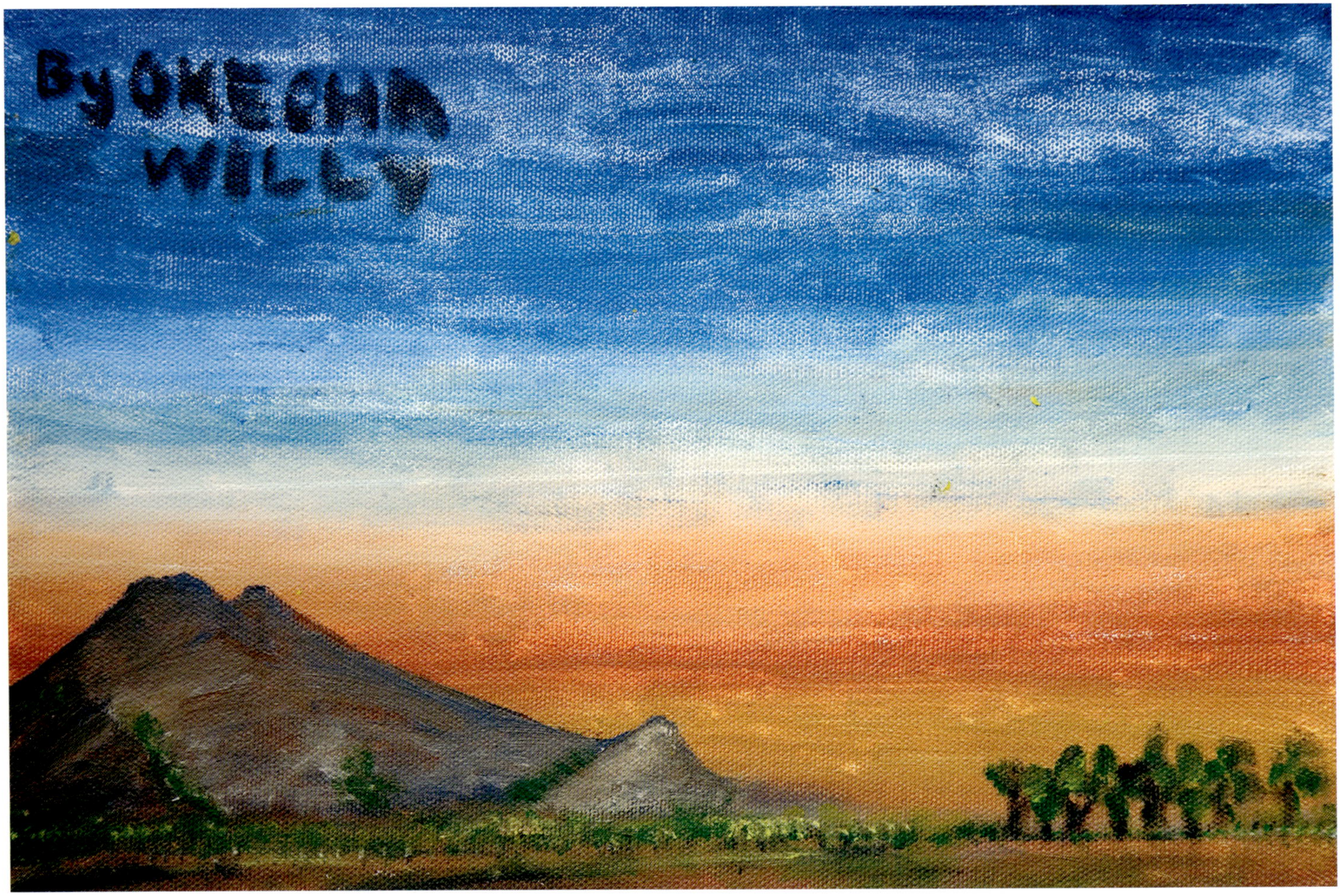
By OKECHA
WILLY

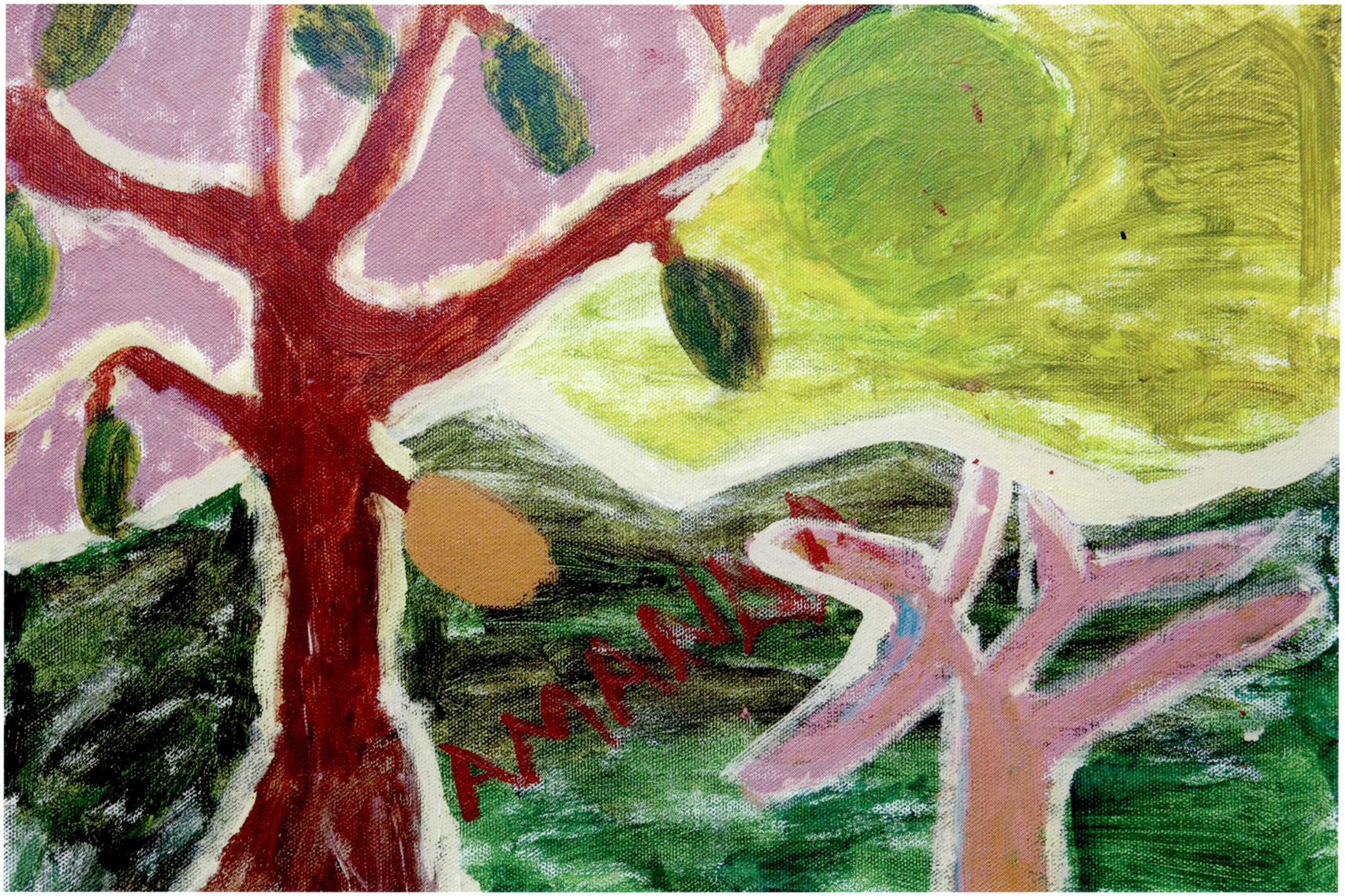
AMAN

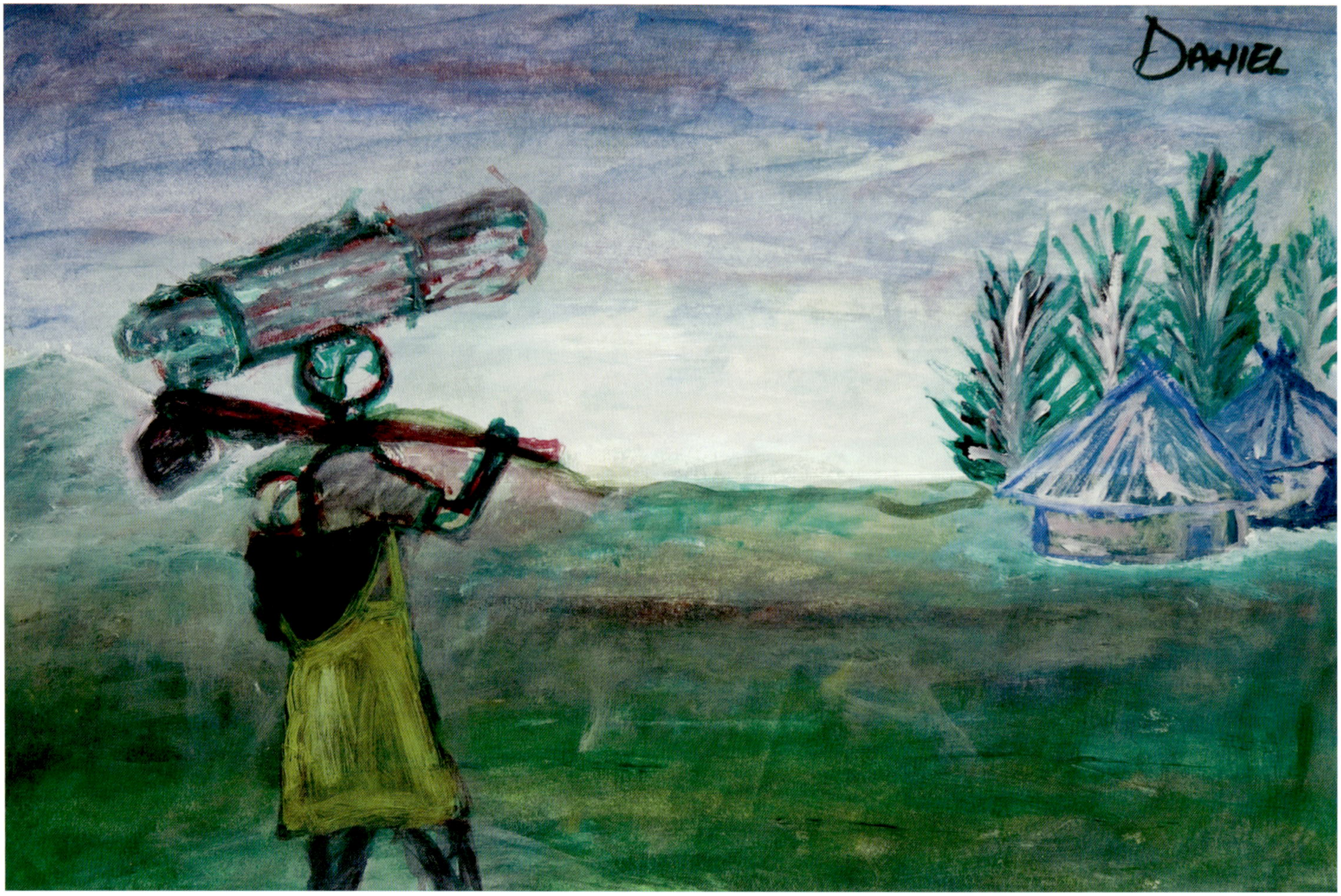
DANIEL

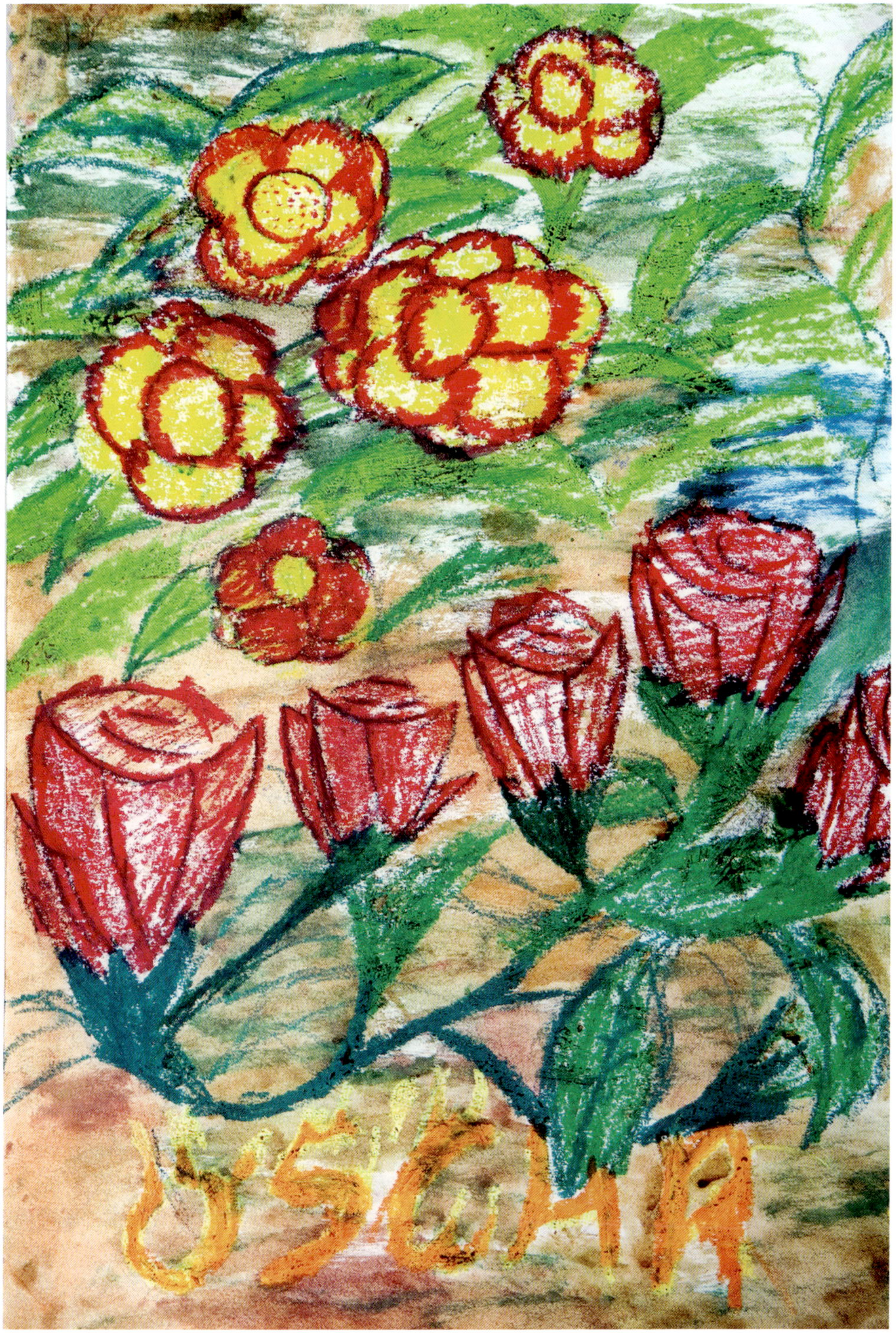
USHA

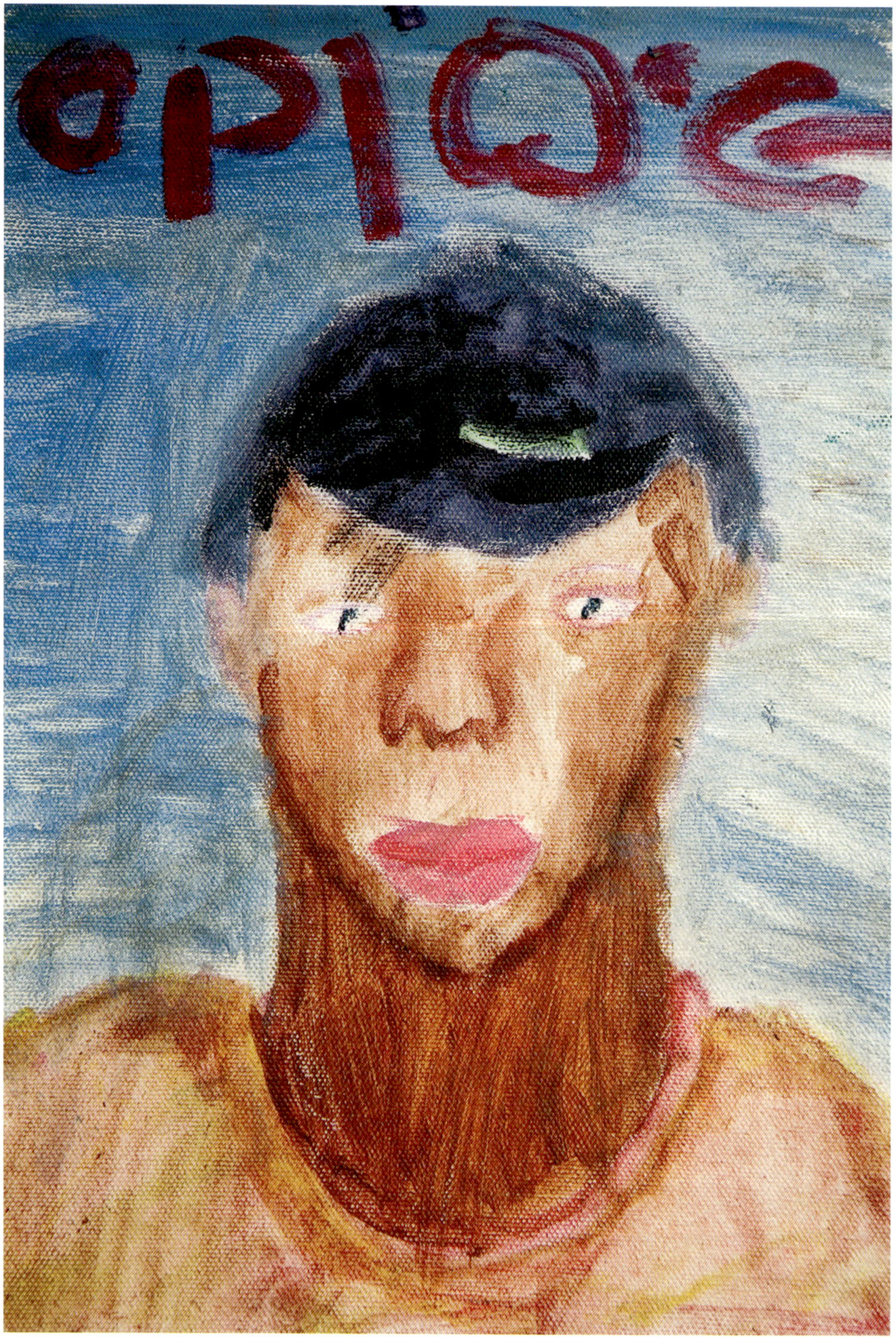

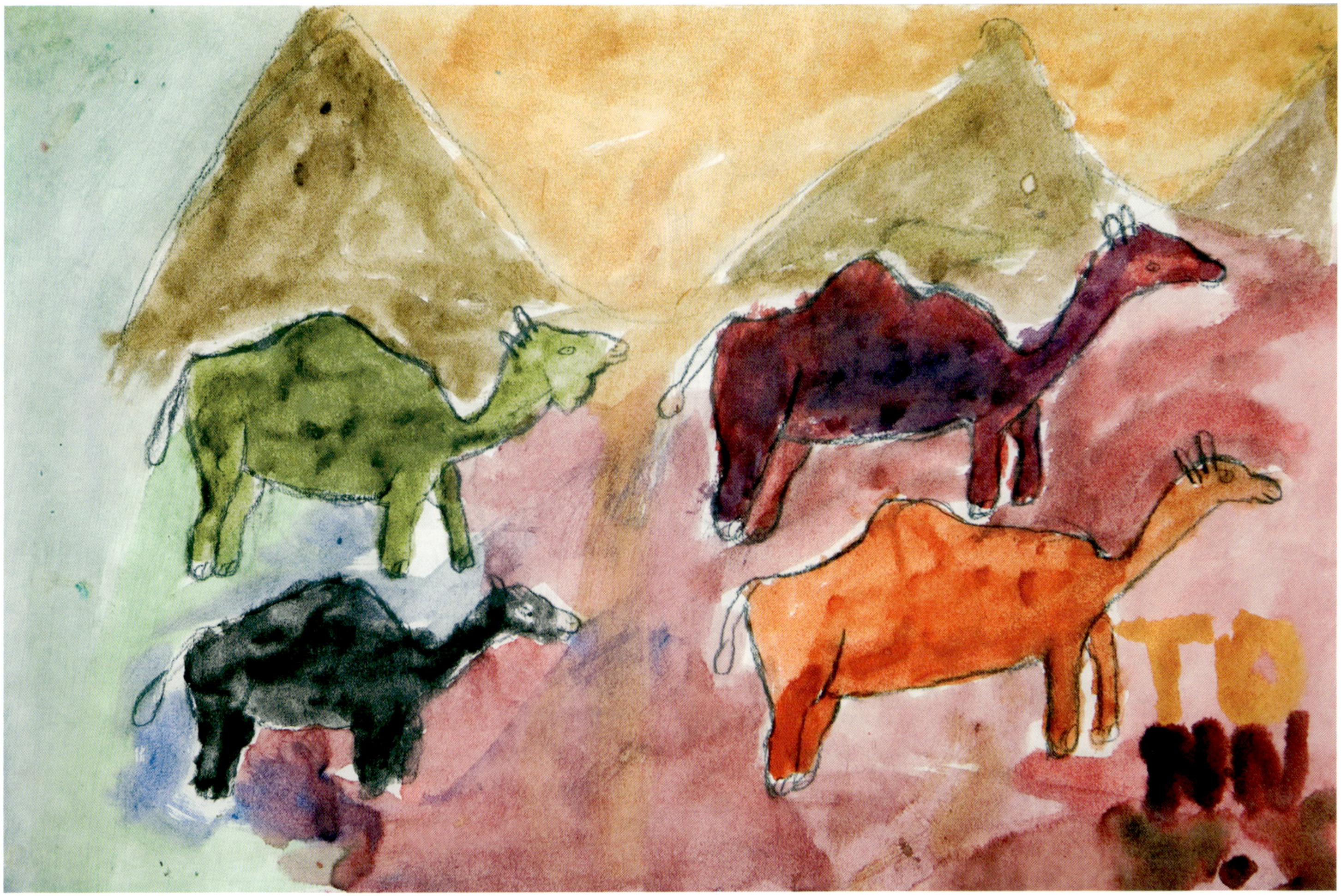
TO

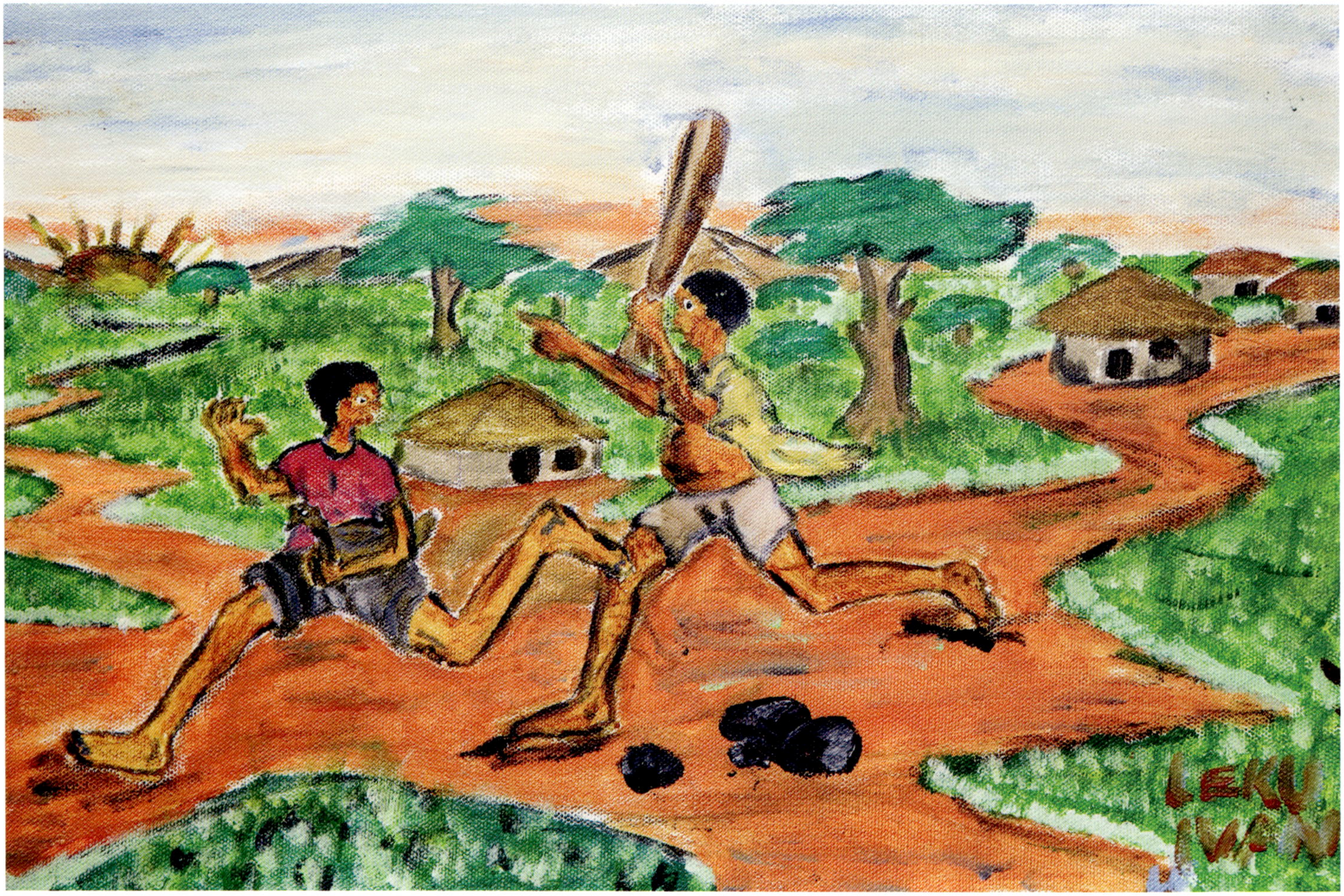
LEKU
IVAN

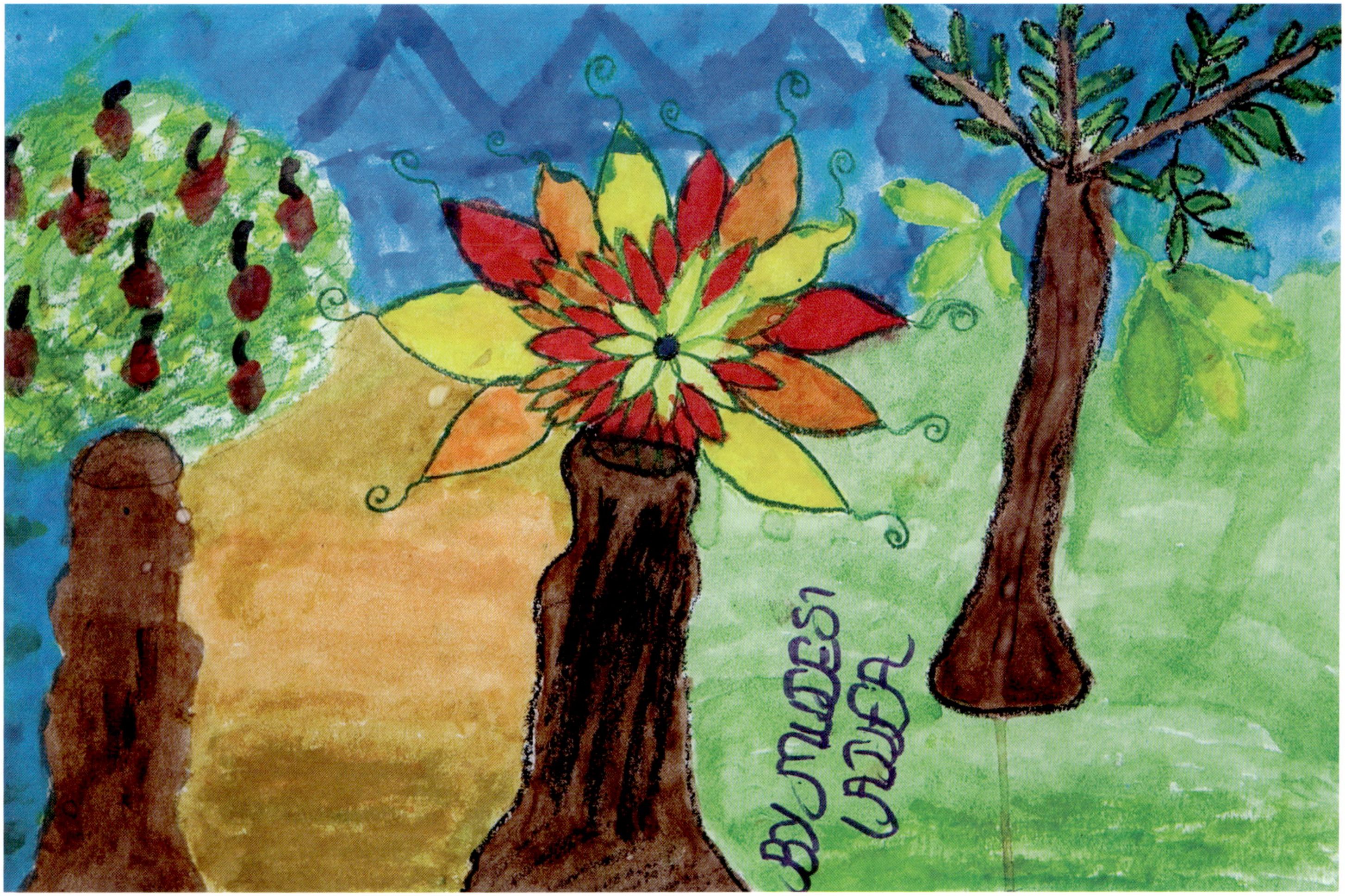
BY MUDESI

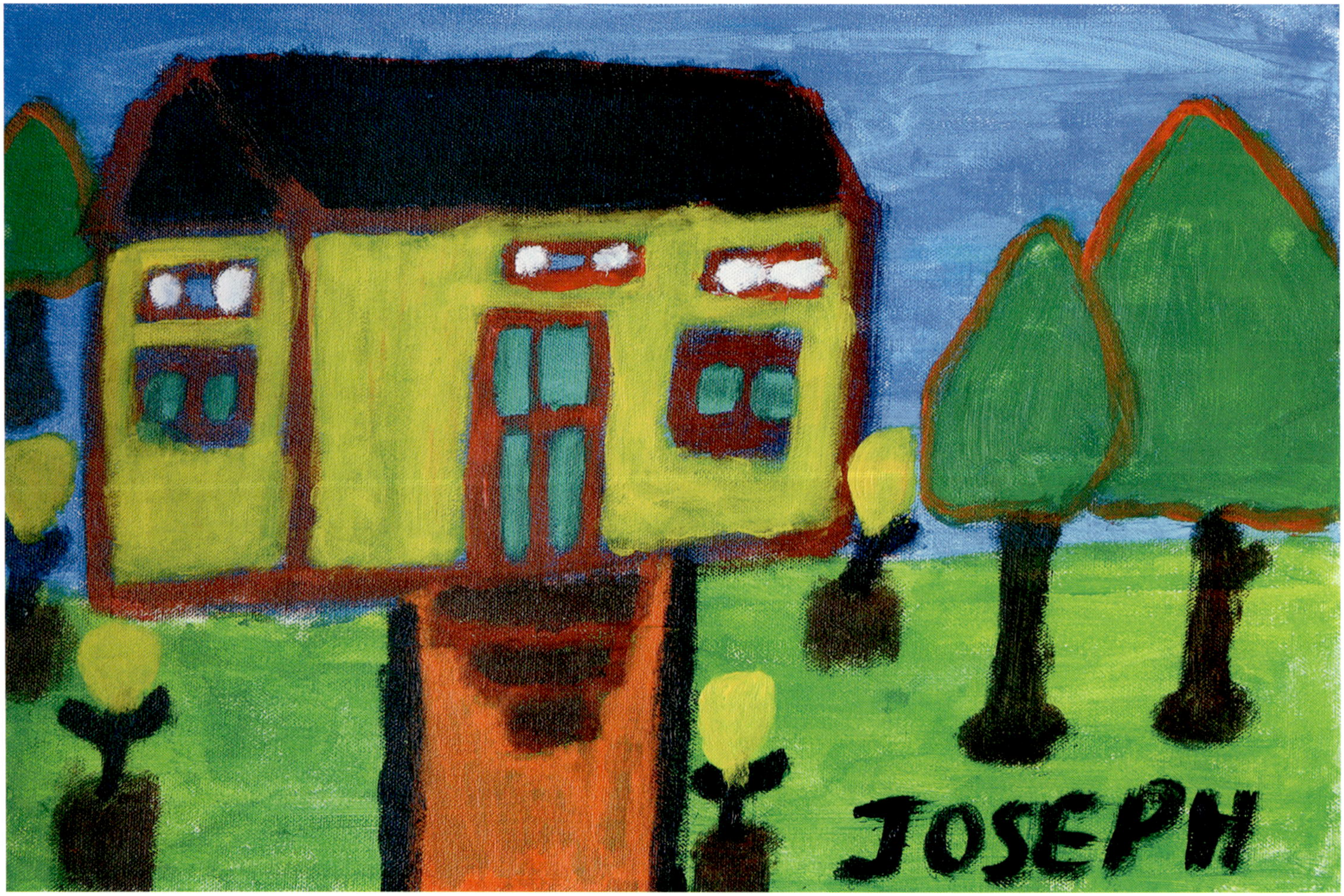
JOSEPH

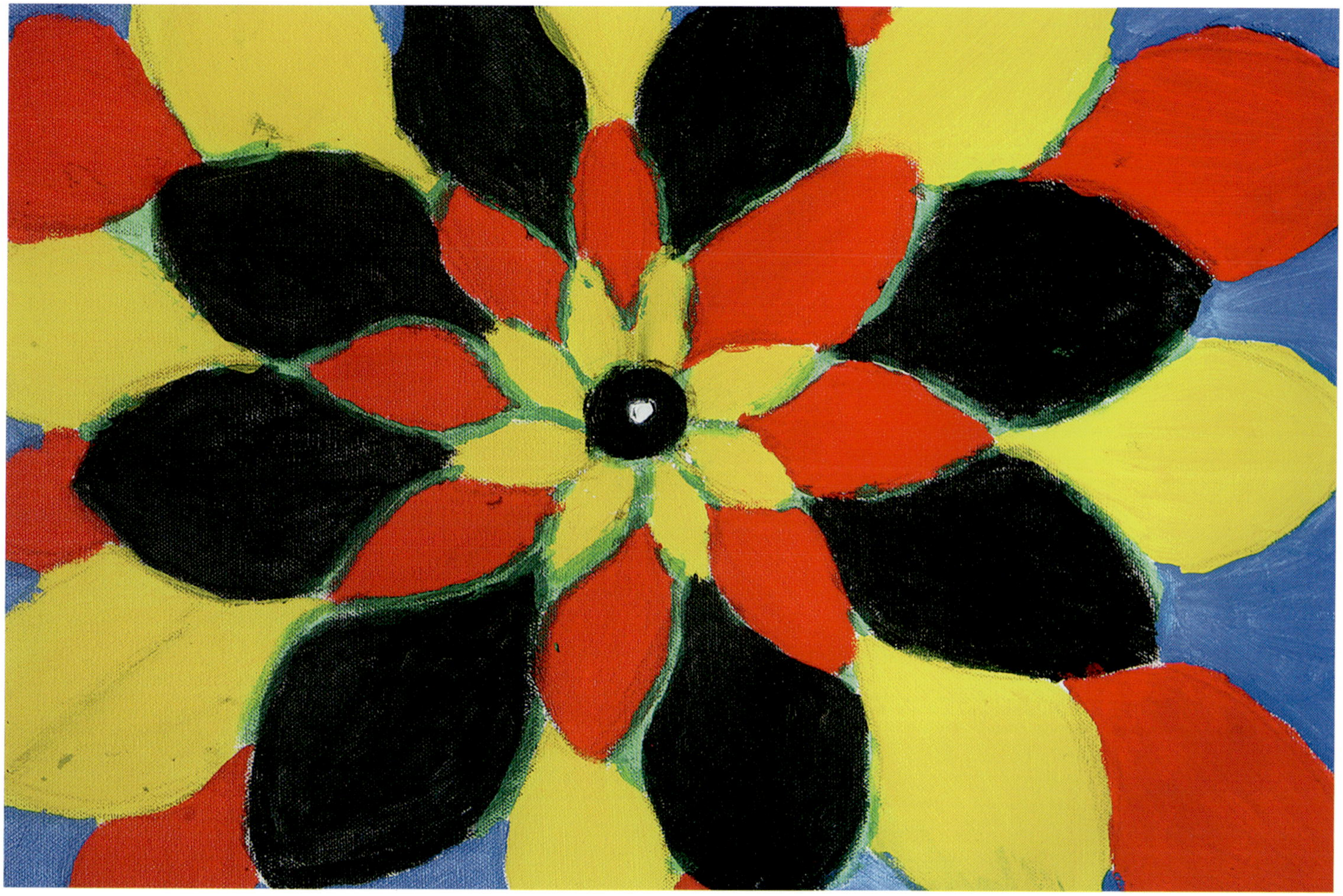

CHANGETHETRUTH.ORG

CHANGE
THE TRUTH
Providing opportunities for Ugandan children

In an effort to reach into myself and then reach out to others, I founded Change the Truth, a not-for-profit, 501(c)(3) organization dedicated to supporting the needs of the children at Saint Mary Kevin Orphanage Motherhood (SMKOM) in Kajjansi, Uganda. SMKOM is home to about 180 orphans and disadvantaged children. It provides shelter, food, security, clothing, medicine, love, access to education and training in vocational skills. The orphanage has few resources because of limited government programs and extremely high poverty levels. Change the Truth provides assistance to the orphanage, placing an emphasis on education, food, medical care, clean water, art/play/music therapy and the support of sustainable activities such as gardening, brick making and pig farming.

The organization has grown from a handful of contributors to a large base of enthusiastic supporters. I would like to thank the board of directors and our many friends who have committed themselves to Change the Truth; together we have been able to make the lives of the children at SMKOM fuller and brighter. It has been a remarkable collaboration.

As has the creation of this book.

The teamwork required to bring it to life has included the children at the orphanage, particularly those who told me about their dreams and who then collaborated with me to make photographs that depicted them. The children who showed up day after day to make paintings and drawings also deserve recognition and appreciation. The staff at the orphanage assisted me at every turn, and I thank them as well, chiefly Rosemary and Joseph Kavulu, Joan Faith Nabulu and Michael Kolulye. I would also like to express deep gratitude to my assistant in Uganda, Peter Damba. Without the honesty, trust, intelligence, ingenuity and enthusiasm of these incredible human beings, this book would not have been possible.

The volunteers who accompanied me on trips to the orphanage in 2007 and 2008 are extraordinary people. I am appreciative of the kindness, generosity, expertise, dedication and passion of Randy Clark, Max Feinstein, Linda Gerstel, Fred Grossman, Carol Joseph, Sarah Joyce, Tom Maddox, Lynne Melcher, Melissa Mosher, Bobbi Newman, Lonnie Powell, Ann Thomas and Jane Voorhees.

Once the seeds for this book were planted, Ann Thomas and Thatcher Hullerman Cook helped give it shape. Lindsay Laricks and Sam Brandao worked magic on its design and editing, respectively. Others who provided assistance include: Keith F. Davis, Adam Freedman, Martha Gershun, Jonathan Ojara and Brian Reisinger. I am indebted to all of these people for their talent, energy and commitment.

My family (Eddie, Abbie, Sam and Max) has been a source of understanding and encouragement each step of the way. I doubt that I will ever be able to thank them enough.

My good friend, Carol Joseph, is the reason this book got printed and found its way into your hands. Because of her, my dream of giving a voice to the children who have touched me so deeply has become a reality.

To all of these people I say *webale nnyo*: thank you very much.

ALL PROCEEDS FROM THE SALE OF THIS BOOK WILL GO DIRECTLY TO CHANGE THE TRUTH AND WILL PROVIDE OPPORTUNITIES FOR TONY AND THE OTHER CHILDREN AT SAINT MARY KEVIN ORPHANAGE MOTHERHOOD.

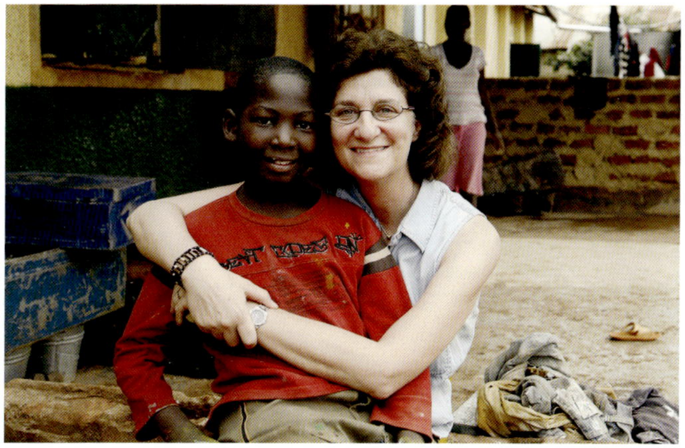

Photo Credit: Melissa Mosher

GLORIA AND TONY, 2008

TITLES (black and white photography)

ARTISTS (drawings and paintings)